Blessings to you
and your family

Jon Huber

THE SOUL OF FAMILY BUSINESS

A practical guide to family business success

and a loving family

TOM HUBLER

LILJA
PRESS

Copyright © 2018 by Tom Hubler
Design and production by:
Lilja Communications, Eden Prairie, Minnesota

Published by Lilja Press
8953 Aztec Drive, Eden Prairie, Minnesota 55347

www.liljapress.com

Library of Congress Cataloging-in-Publication Data

Hubler, Tom
The Soul of Family Business
A practical guide to family business success and a loving family/Tom Hubler
ISBN: 978-0-578-26108-9
Library of Congress Control Number: 2018953900
Printed in the United States of America
First printing September 2018

Early praise for *The Soul of Family Business*

While nothing tops the value and impact of interacting with a family business consultant face-to-face, this book is a wonderful source of practical tools and thoughtful reflections tested over a lifetime of Tom's consulting work. It is a candy store of delights, of lessons, for people involved with business families of every age and stage.

—Bill Monson, former director of the
University of St. Thomas Family Business Center

Drawing from the depths of his personal and professional experience, Tom Hubler guides us through the life cycles, challenges, and opportunities of family business. His inspirational anecdotes and wisdom-filled one-liners could only come from the experience of a highly respected senior practitioner. Spiritually grounded, they are designed to stimulate thought, reflection, and action for family business owners and practitioners alike. He does not simply visit the world of family business; with a philosopher's insight, he probes its depths.

—Paul Karofsky, founder of Transition
Consulting Group, Ltd., executive director emeritus of
Northeastern University's Center for Family Business,
author of *So You're in the Family Business:
A Guide to Sustainability*, and a
third-generation family business owner

If you are an owner of a family business or consult to one, *The Soul of Family Business* is a must-read. Webster's dictionary defines soul as "the immaterial essence, animating principle, or actuating cause of an individual life." Tom Hubler does not disappoint the reader; there is no part of the family business soul that Tom does not address. From love, values, gratitude, forgiveness, and conflict to succession, family health, and more. Every issue discussed is followed by one or more mini case studies. This is a hands-on book that captures Tom's many years of dealing with family businesses.

—August Aquila,
CEO of AQUILA Global Advisors, LLC

This book has great insights into the inner workings of family business by one of the top consultants in the field.

—Gary B. Cohen, managing partner of CO2 Partners
and author of *Just Ask Leadership:
Why great managers always ask the right questions*

Tom is one of very few pioneers in the professional field of family business consulting. I've had the privilege of knowing and learning from Tom for over 20 years, and in *The Soul of Family Business*, Tom shares his deeply rooted experience working with business families. Through his consulting experiences, references to the insights he's gained from his mentors and teachers, and sharing of the step-by-step interventions of his work, Tom has provided families and practitioners alike with wisdom for the ages.

Tom is a deeply soulful individual. This long overdue treatise reflects Tom's soulful essence of his life's work. Reading *The Soul of Family Business* is to express our gratitude for Tom's immense contributions to the field.

—Mark B. Rubin, senior managing director
of FTI Consulting and founding partner of
The Metropolitan Group LLC

The Soul of Family Business offers practical tips and advice, allowing readers to choose what will work best for their business families. His Inside-Out Succession Plan model is simple, pragmatic and achievable; it captures the essence of his work with legacy business families. The book is a great primer for anyone involved in family businesses—from owners and family members to non-family managers and external advisors. Hubler has lived family business both personally and professionally, and he shares his knowledge generously. His book is a valuable, insightful gift to all business families and their advisors.

—Aron R. Pervin, founder of Optimizer720 and
family business consultant at
Pervin Family Business Advisors Inc.

Tom is a true sage in the field of family business. In reading this book, Tom brings out the soul and essence of what it means to be a family business. He describes in-depth all the issues that are so pertinent to family businesses. It is a must-read for all family business consultants!

—Carmen Bianchi, founder of Carmen Bianchi
Family Business Associates and founder and
former director of the EMC Business Forum at
San Diego State University and the
University of Texas at El Paso Family Business Forum

I am very fortunate to have been a part of Tom's work for over 30 years. He has helped me in my professional career, as well as in my relationships with family and friends. He has expertly captured his lifelong vocation and identified the soul of family and family business in this book. Reading *The Soul of Family Business* will help you be a more thoughtful consultant, a more successful business owner and, most importantly, a better person.

—Thomas E. Zanecchia, president of
Wealth Management Consultants, Inc.

The Soul of Family Business is the best guide to keeping your family and your business well grounded. As a CPA, I have seen how the crossroads of family and business need to be intentionally navigated to be successful. As Tom says, "it's easier to prevent a problem than to try to fix one."

—John Lawson, CPA and shareholder at
Schechter Dokken Kanter CPAs

Rooted in his upbringing, education and decades of experience, Tom Hubler has crafted his own style in helping business families reach their goals. *The Soul of Family Business* presents the tools, methods and examples for finding harmony and success in both the business and family, and shows the inner workings of how Tom helps clients find solutions they didn't know existed.

—Jon Keimig, director of the
University of St. Thomas Family Business Center

The Soul of Family Business is a masterpiece packed with wisdom and stories from one of the pioneers of family business consulting. Business owners and consultants alike will benefit from Tom's deep understanding of the intricacies of running a successful family business.

—Dave Wondra, president of Wondra Group LLC and past global chairman of International Coach Federation

When I met Tom, too many years ago to count, I was impressed with his values, insight, sensitivity, and understanding of the problems and paths to resolution for members of family businesses. I was an associate editor of the *Family Business Review* at the time, and what he was saying was far more thoughtful than most of what was being written and researched—I daresay it still is! I knew his message had to reach a larger audience, so I encouraged him to write and publish to help advance the field. I am grateful that he did, and certainly this book is in line with all Tom is. All who are interested in deeper understanding of family business should read *The Soul of Family Business.*

—Joseph Astrachan, Wells Fargo Eminent Scholar Chair of Family Business and past executive director of the Cox Family Enterprise Center at Kennesaw State University, author, and coeditor of the *Journal of Family Business Strategy*

This book is all about creating and preserving a truly healthy family in business. Unlike most family business literature, this book's focus is not best practices but rather the heart and soul of the family in business. Conflict resolution, recovery from substance abuse and family betrayals, forgiveness, and gratitude are elegantly and practically discussed in Thomas Hubler's *The Soul of Family Business.*

—Ernesto J. Poza, founder of family-business.com, professor emeritus at Thunderbird School of Global Management, and co-author of *Family Business*

Tom Hubler, as "dean" of family business advisors, has filled a craftsman's chest of tools worn smooth by generations of use. Tom generously shares priceless gifts—the family forgiveness ritual for new beginnings and stories of problems avoided by structure and formality. Family businesses and advisors will prosper using this practical wisdom.

—Steve Coleman, partner of Platinum Group

Is there a "secret sauce" for family business survival? With more than 20 years of experience advising family businesses, Tom Hubler describes stunning transformations within businesses and families as they discover the soul that drives their family business. Hubler makes the case that the secret sauce that differentiates successful family businesses from others is a combination of values, purpose, and yes, love. Together, these factors create a soul that helps families surmount difficulties embedded in every family and energizes family members to work hard, solve problems, and believe in a cause greater than oneself—the family business.

Hubler explains that soul is also crucial to these businesses because of the unique fluid boundaries between family and business. Unlike non-family businesses, family members of family businesses may be tempted to dominate family gatherings, dinners, or even while brushing teeth, with work-related discussions. While these mutable boundaries can be helpful in conveying information quickly, they can also be overpowering and lead to dissonance. According to Hubler, the family's soul can help families determine when business discussions should be allowed to permeate family interactions, and when they should be banned.

Most enlightening, Hubler demonstrates through case studies that soul determines the success of governance policies. When decisions surrounding business strategies and goals, or rules concerning family members' rights (such as buy-sell agreements and family employment) are based on values and purpose, they are more likely to stick.

Hubler's book should be read by all family business owners, their families, and associates. His message about soul as the family's secret sauce may sound un-businesslike, but in fact, can be a family business's most powerful ally.

—Kathy Overbeke, founder of GPS: Generation Planning Strategies, LLC and a family business consultant

In *The Soul of Family Business*, Tom Hubler provides family business owners with important insights and processes to help them build a better future for their families and businesses. He shows compassion and respect for each family's integrity as they navigate the balance between owning a company and having long-standing, often complicated relationships with one another. The book describes the hard work and dedication required and offers cases and practical exercises to face the challenges.

—Lilli Friedland, president of Executive Advisors

By sharing his 30+ years of seasoned insights, coupled with actual case studies to beautifully illustrate the concepts, Tom Hubler has written a book that is an instant classic for family businesses of all kinds. More than 15 years ago, Tom did a wonderful job of bringing our multi-generation family closer together as individuals and as a team, helping us become better family shareholders and preparing us to meet future challenges. *The Soul of Family Business* reflects Tom's consulting style, one that encourages family members to speak up and be heard, to feel secure and be listened to, and to be motivated and tested in achieving goals. Your family—like ours—will be better for having benefitted from Tom Hubler's wisdom.

—Richard Murphy, president and CEO of
Murphy Warehouse Company

Tom Hubler has written a reference book for family business leaders who need a "wisdom resource," a collection of sound principles and teachings from an experienced elder intended to spark their own ideas on how to help their family move forward—in both their responsibilities to the future of the family business and in their cultivation of love for each other.

Hubler emphasizes that in order to build an enduring company, business families must master two kinds of skill: proactive skills to prevent divisive, painful conflict; and skills to heal and move forward when such conflicts occur. But what makes this book special is the author's collected gems of wisdom about how to initiate productive family conversations, so that when conflict happens, there can be respectful attention to resolution, personal healing and renewed commitment.

Using case studies from his own experience, Hubler describes practical ways to initiate constructive conversation among family members to discuss issues that affect their ability to work together. He describes ways to initiate forgiveness practices within the family so that personal hurt, harm or betrayal can be acknowledged and corrected with care and respect.

—Allen Bettis, president of Legacy Associates
Family Business Advisors

For decades, Tom has been both an ardent student and teacher of families in business. This exemplary book is testimony to Tom's passion and skills in building healthy families and strong family businesses.

—Paddy McNeely, CEO of Meritex Enterprises

Dedication

I dedicate this book to my "real" editor and loving wife, Joy, whose critique, continuous support, and love have created the soul of our relationship.

Table of Contents

Foreword

When people ask me how I got into family business consulting, there are two answers I give. The official one is that I was a professional therapist who grew interested in the challenges families faced in running businesses together while maintaining their essential family relationships—father to daughter, mother to son, grandfather to grandson, and so on.

The unofficial answer is that I started as an unpaid volunteer therapist in my own family at age seven. Because my own family was troubled, I became a mediator almost as soon as I could talk. Ever since then, I've been on a quest to create happy families, starting with my own. I've simply professionalized it and made a career out of it.

But as I've gotten more deeply involved in my work with families and their businesses, it has been like peeling back an onion to reach the essential root of both the family and its business—something I call the "soul" of family business.

According to the *Oxford English Dictionary*[i]*, "soul" is defined as the essence or embodiment of something, whether it is a person or quality, such as "the soul of discretion" (which, by the way, is a useful quality to have in a family business!).

For many years I have been talking about "soul" in individual sessions with my client families, in speeches, and in the many articles I've written for business publications. Increasingly, I've incorporated the concept into my family business consulting work with more than five hundred families over the past three decades. I've

* Please see References section for information on statistics and cited material in each chapter.

explained it and helped others to understand it, sometimes across seemingly large generational divides. Joyfully, I have experienced firsthand the rewards that come from its expression within a family-owned business.

This lifelong exploration has led me to write the book you are now holding in your hands. There are many books written about family businesses and their unique challenges and opportunities, but *The Soul of Family Business* is different in that I prefer to look at the topic through a different lens.

Family businesses are certainly deserving of attention. Today, family-held businesses comprise eighty to ninety percent of all enterprises in the United States and account for more than sixty percent of the country's GDP. Yet less than one-third (thirty percent) of families control their businesses into the second generation, and only about twelve percent make it into the third generation.[ii]

There are many different families involved in business enterprises today, from small mom-and-pop retail stores to multinational corporations. No matter the size or scope of a family enterprise, I've seen that families with soul qualities embedded within their businesses generally are able to identify their soul, and they live those values for the benefit of their family and the success of the company. Some families ignore or are unable to identify their soul, and as a consequence, they do not thrive. But having a close reflection of soul helps family members thrive within their businesses, and it not only generates capital and wealth but also happiness and career satisfaction in equal measure.

The soul of a family business has to do with the family's values, love, and heritage. It has to do with everything that's happened in the family, both the good and bad things alike, that creates the essence of who they are. I like to call this their "secret sauce" that makes them unique and fuels their success. That secret sauce is what families need to bottle because it's what differentiates them from all other businesses, family-owned and not.

In my consulting work, we often begin by asking: "What are the family values that you would like to see perpetuated in your business?" We then use those values to craft a Common Family Vision™ designed to help to unite all family members. That becomes their inspiration, and as they articulate what they want for themselves and for others within and outside the business, it's under the umbrella of this family vision.

The question is often posed: Are you a business first or a family first? I've always said it's business first, but with a major family emphasis—so it isn't either/or. It's a business with a family vision attached to it, and when executed and embraced correctly it represents a powerful combination.

In this book, I'll talk about how family businesses must satisfy the **B.O.S.S.**, a concept advanced by Sherod Miller[iii] that I have found to be very helpful (more on this in Chapter 2).

We'll look at the foundation of family business, including how love factors into it. We'll examine the elements of soul in the business and look at best practices, as well. We'll take a look at the lifecycle inherent in a family business, from learning the business, doing the business, and teaching the business to letting go of the business. We'll examine how the entrepreneur is highly skilled at running the business and how it can represent a great deal of his or her self-image. We'll look at how conflicts can erupt as the younger generation begins to run the business while the entrepreneur is letting go of it—and how various mindfulness and forgiveness practices can facilitate each phase.

We'll look at the Last Challenge of Entrepreneurship™, which not only involves passing the torch to next-generation family owners but also finding new pursuits and dreams for the entrepreneur once he or she has left the business.

Sprinkled throughout are stories from my own experiences working with clients, since these real situations have informed my work and theories. For longer stories, you will see them sectioned off with the title, "From the Case Study Files." In all cases, the names and other identifying details have been changed to protect client confidentiality.

I also will share what I call the Hubler Checklist™ (see page 16), which provides a list of topics that are important to family businesses, from the benefits of family meetings to useful skills for family business members to employ, such as listening and forgiveness.

In the final chapter, the section titled "Family Business Consultants as Leaders" (page 165) is designed to help the professionals who work with family-owned firms be more effective with their family business clients. My emphasis is on shedding light on issues and eliminating the shadows that can derail family-owned enterprises. And even though the chapter is written for outside professionals, members of family businesses can read this chapter, too, to help them evaluate the quality and character of the consultants they may be working with in their family businesses.

As I round the corner into the endgame of my life, I am happy to share what I've learned with others. It's my hope that it will help members of family businesses appreciate their uniqueness. It's my hope that it will help prevent an unspoken issue—a mere speck of dust—from derailing an entire family and their business. And it's my hope that other professionals may benefit from some of the small insights they read here.

Because when all is said and done, it has been my honor and privilege to work with some of the most amazing people—families like yours—who have created enterprises that not only support their families but others' families, as well—and make the world a better place.

Tom Hubler
Saint Paul, Minnesota

1

THE FOUNDATION OF FAMILY BUSINESS

The story goes that a father and son are sitting in the hot tub on a Friday evening.

The father says, "I'm sorry things haven't worked out in the family business, but I'm going to have to let you go."

"I'm shocked," says the son.

The father responds, "Speaking as your dad, let me just say how sorry I am to learn you've just lost your job, and I want to do everything I can to help you."

The Business

The entrepreneurial spirit runs high in today's society. People want to go into business for themselves for numerous reasons, whether it be to have the freedom of being their own boss, to increase their earning potential, or simply because they have an idea no one else has ever had. However, while many people are ready to go into business for themselves, few think about starting a family business. Most family businesses are started by an entrepreneur who, over time, brings his or her family members into the business based on skill and trust level. These businesses encompass multiple members of the family and have the capacity to be passed on from generation to generation.

Even at my own firm, Hubler/Swartz (a family business consultancy that I started in 1981 with lawyer Steve Swartz), we operated in that informal way, and it is where I got my first real-life lessons in family business.

One year, the office manager asked me if my daughter, Kirsten, would like to share the receptionist position with another high school student during the summer. As it turned out, she wasn't available, so I asked the office manager if my son, Jon, could take the position instead. She asked if Jon, who was fifteen at the time, was too young to handle the responsibilities of the job, but I asked her to interview him. That evening at home, I mentioned the receptionist job to Jon, and he became excited about the opportunity, especially since it paid more than the fast food industry.

Jon was hired on a one-day probationary period, but he worked the entire summer, answering the phone, doing light typing, and correcting some testing. On the day it was announced that Jon would be working in the company, I said to myself, "I hope he doesn't embarrass me, I hope he works hard, and I hope he doesn't act at the office like he does at home."

Back at home, Kirsten complained. She felt that Jon had taken "her" job. And to fan the flames, Jon would tell Kirsten that I had taken him to visit a client or out to lunch. Kirsten was clearly hurt by her brother's remarks, and, in retrospect, I'm sure she felt emotionally eclipsed by her younger brother.

You can imagine what it was like for me to be in the middle of that situation. Despite my family business consulting background, this was my first personal experience balancing family and business. Even today, my life is a balancing act. My wife, Joy, works with me and handles the administrative functions for our company, Hubler for Business Families. Even though love is at the core of our relationship, the boundaries between business and personal sometimes become blurred.

In an ideal world, an entrepreneur would start his or her family business with a plan to organize the business with proper structure and formality.

But it just doesn't work that way.

When it comes to starting a business, it is not usually the entrepreneur's intention to start a family business. Actually, it usually starts with an idea or a product in the entrepreneur's garage. I've had multiple clients who have grown their small start-up businesses into very successful companies. One small bit of success leads to another, and before they know it, they've outgrown the garage and need to move to a larger space.

Given the informality of the initial structure, it is no surprise that some of the early employees and other members of the family business work for little or no pay—it's their sweat equity that keeps the company afloat. It's also not unusual for an entrepreneur's spouse to do the bookkeeping in a start-up business, and the kids are often eager to help out by emptying wastebaskets or mowing the company's lawn. It's clearly a labor of love for the whole family. At this stage of business development, survival is the most important element, and everyone pitches in to help the company succeed.

Recently I had a client family in the real estate business describe themselves as "urban farmers." They saw themselves like a farm family, where everyone pitches in at an early age to help with the chores.

As a company grows, it is not unusual for the family to become more formally employed. It is a great way to live out family values, create opportunity, and teach the next generation the meaning of work. Even at a young age, the children begin to aspire to someday sit in their mom or dad's chair.

As a family business grows and becomes more successful, there is a need to add structure and formality to preserve the love within a family. In any case, whether you are a start-up family or a more mature family business, managing the family and business boundaries are essential to your success. Coupled with that is the importance of maintaining your family love, which as the business grows will evolve and become the foundation of the soul of your family business.

Lessons from *Fences*

> *"Your dad tried to teach you all the things that he wasn't,*
> *and at the same time you became all of the things that he was."*
> August Wilson, *Fences* (1985)

In his award-winning play *Fences*, August Wilson comments on what is considered a common dynamic between fathers and sons: tension and competition. The play features Troy Maxim, a father who grew up playing baseball in the Negro Leagues and who is a victim of racism in many aspects of his life—he is bitter and resentful. With almost unrelenting bombasity, he's at war with the racism that has boxed him in his whole life. To offset his experiences of racism, Troy builds a fence in his backyard to protect his son and keep the effects of racism from impacting his family.

Troy's son, Cory, has a future that rests on getting a football scholarship. Troy's pride, jealousy, and concern for the white man's impact on his son causes him to meddle with Cory's future, and sadly the son does not get the scholarship. Cory is angry with his father, stops speaking to him, and, in reaction, enters the armed services.

Did this famous playwright promote a stereotype? A stereotype is generally defined as a widely held but fixed or oversimplified idea of a type of person or thing. My dictionary includes the pejorative, "to make hackneyed."

The stereotypical father runs the business, puts bread on the table, and is both the family and company CEO. Continuing this business family stereotype, the mother is also the CEO: Chief Emotional Officer. Maybe that's hackneyed and outdated, but in my experience, that has been true of family-run businesses; happily, I am now seeing more female entrepreneurs and daughters being groomed to take over family businesses.

Back to fathers, I have realized over years of consulting just how vital fathers are in the emotional development of their adult sons and daughters. Fathers who take the time to bless their children by participating in their lives recognize the powerful bond that is created. The fathers' investment of time and energy reaps tremendous rewards in the relationships they enjoy with their sons and daughters.

Sons who are the beneficiaries of their fathers' attention are generally much more successful. Similarly, when fathers bless their daughters with attention, the daughters tend to do better in school, particularly in math, science, and business.

Troubled father/son or father/daughter business relationships that make the news are often directly related to what has or has not happened in the parent-child relationship. Tension in the business relationship often results from the emotional deficit that accrued in the family between the father and the children.

That fathers are critical to the emotional development of their sons and daughters is likely no surprise. But even when deficits in emotional involvement have occurred, it is never too late in the family business to make an adjustment. Fathers should (may I say "must"?) get involved now with their adult children and their grandchildren. It is mutually rewarding, heals past hurts, and prevents future business/leadership tensions.

Part of the reason to emphasize the role of fathers in an emotional sense is to offset the role of mothers as the CEO (Chief Emotional Officer). Not only does the moniker stereotype mothers and diminish their role in the family business, it also enables fathers to operate within their own stereotype and focus solely on business, regardless of family emotions. Truly authentic fathers and mothers both provide emotional input and love to their families.

Supportive spouses in family business have historically been female, though there are some notable exceptions. Bill Ramirez not only supported his entrepreneurial wife, Mary Louisa Ramirez, the founder of a Mexican food company that manufactured tortillas, he also provided most of the technical experience for their company. Mary Louisa had grown up in a family business and came into her entrepreneurial spirit naturally. She and Bill worked together, though he eventually left due to family conflict. What made Mary Louisa special and unique was that no one in her family had formal training in the food industry; they learned the business by trial and error—from the ground up. Mary Louisa also honed her business skills, eventually negotiating a major partnership with a national supplier—the first and only time that supplier was a minority partner in such a deal.

Mary Louisa's three children eventually joined the business. They moved into roles that matched their gifts and made positive contributions to the company. Mary Louisa groomed her oldest son, Mario, to manage the financials and her younger son, José, to manage equipment and maintenance. It was her daughter, Diana, with her formal business training and managerial experience, whom Mary Louisa groomed to eventually replace herself.

Another example is Mary Lilja, an entrepreneur and the editor of this book. Mary grew up in a family business in which she says the business "was like the fifth sibling around the dinner table each evening," where business topics were often discussed. During college, each child worked summer stints in the business, and while her brothers ultimately were able to work there, she pursued a corporate career. Honing her entrepreneurial spirit, however, she started her own public relations and book publishing business, combining her corporate experience with the knowledge she had gleaned from her father. Consistent with the model of spouses being supportive to their entrepreneurial partners, Mary's husband, Mike, has provided IT and accounting functions for the company, as well as being a critical advisor since the beginning. The company, now 30 years and counting, also employs their daughter, Kate.

In a typical and strategic model, the spouse often becomes the primary advisor and major confidant to the entrepreneur. From a systems perspective, the spouse is the stabilizing force in the system—offering stability in their personal and business relationships, which allows the entrepreneur to take the risks that he or she does. At the same time, the spouse provides solace when the business experiences setbacks and acts as the cheerleader when successes occur.

The same is true in my relationship with my wife, Joy, who provides most of the administrative function for my consulting work. More importantly, she acts as my sounding board when I'm perplexed about a difficult client situation. Her insight and professional guidance allow me an opportunity to reflect and create alternate methods to address client issues. I would be lost without her—I wasn't kidding when I mentioned in the book dedication that she is my real-life editor!

Building Emotional Connections

In my experience, I've worked with many male family business leaders, and I have realized over years of consulting just how vital fathers are in the emotional development of their adult sons and daughters. Fathers who take the time to bless their children by participating in their lives recognize the powerful bond that is created. A father's investment of time and energy reaps tremendous rewards in the relationships he enjoys with his sons and daughters.

There are so many opportunities with your grandchildren to share your values and help the younger generation understand what is important to you and what motivates you to do what you do. I have found a great way to build emotional connections that are fun and natural: I hold an annual film festival for my two (now fifteen-year-old) grandsons who are cousins. Last year, the film festival theme was 1930/1940s genre horror films, e.g., *Frankenstein*, *The Wolf Man*, and *Dracula*. While this may sound intense, the weekend included lots of pizza, swimming, and a local fireworks display. The theme for this year's festival focused on father-son relationships. We watched *Captains Courageous, The Red Pony,* and *Shane.* In each film, the son is neglected or held at an emotional distance from his father.

In *Captains Courageous,* the father and son are completely alienated. The son is a spoiled, entitled brat who is kicked out of prep school. The father is a business tycoon immersed in his business dealings. The story is about how the boy's life is transformed when he is lost at sea and then rescued by a fisherman who teaches him about life skills, values, and manhood through fishing. The boy and his father connect emotionally at the end of the film while the boy is grieving over the loss of his fisherman friend and mentor.

A similar dynamic occurs in *The Red Pony,* in which a father and son are distant. To connect with his son, the father gives the boy a red pony. However, the son learns about life, values, and manhood from the family's hired hand. At the close of the film, the father becomes involved in his son's emotional life, and they finally share a connection.

In *Shane,* the father and son are not alienated, but the son idolizes a transient, retired gunfighter from whom he learns about life, values, and manhood.

Each of these stories could have just as easily been about a father and his daughter. Together they demonstrate that when the father or his surrogate becomes emotionally involved with a child, the child is better able to learn life lessons.

However you choose to spend time with your children and grandchildren, use these shared times to explore your relationships and your expectations of one another. As Neil Chethik mentions in his book *Fatherloss* (2001)[i], it takes time to share the words you always wanted to hear: "I love you. I appreciate you, and I admire the life you are leading."

In the same way, adult children can take the initiative and act on their expectations. A friend of mine recently commented that his relationship with his father was not affectionate enough. When his father was diagnosed with early-onset Alzheimer's disease, my friend realized that he had to change the relationship to become more affectionate. Now whenever he greets his father, it's the father who initiates the hug.

In *Fences*, Troy, the father, dies while his son is away serving in the armed forces. When Cory, the son, returns home at the time of his father's death and refuses to attend the funeral, his mother says to him, "Your dad tried to teach you all the things that he wasn't, and at the same time you became all of the things that he was."

Reach out to your family members, break down your emotional fences, and offer a hug or a kiss. Get involved in one another's emotional lives. It makes good sense, and your actions will go right to the bottom line.

The Power of Love

> *What's love got to do, got to do with it*
> *What's love but a second hand emotion*
> *What's love got to do, got to do with it*
> *Who needs a heart when a heart can be broken.*
> Tina Turner, "What's Love Got to Do With It"

Success in a family business is a lot about love. That begs the question (as Tina Turner asked), What's Love Got to Do With It? My answer is simple: Everything!

Love is the foundation of a productive and successful business family. The closeness of family is what separates those who own a business from all other work relationships. The entanglement of business and family complicates the work environment because it is difficult to balance work with family. Family life and work life intertwine, so there's no place to hide when there is stress in one or the other.

The crossover can easily overwhelm individuals. Friction causes pain and isolation. Disagreements get personal. There's no way to get away. I believe the answer is disarmingly but deceptively simple: Love. Regularly demonstrated among family members, love is the foundation of a productive, successful business family. I saw it unfold firsthand between two brothers and their family business.

◼ FROM THE CASE STUDY FILES: BROTHERS IN CONFLICT

John and Carl grew up in their family's manufacturing business. John became an integral part of the business right after he graduated high school. He sacrificed his college career to help his father complete crucial government contracts that greatly enhanced the business.

Carl was able to go to college and earn a business degree. After graduating, he traveled around Europe for the summer. When he returned from his three-month European holiday, his father, Frank, recruited Carl into the business. He joined at the same pay level as his brother, John, and they both held titles of vice president.

John was deeply hurt. He felt taken for granted. For two years his unhappiness festered until he couldn't take it anymore. John left the family business, moved across the river to Wisconsin, and started his own company as a direct competitor. All communication broke down; John no longer had contact with his family.

Years passed. Children were born who didn't meet their cousins. Both businesses thrived, but John and his wife and children never ventured across the river for family gatherings or holidays.

One cold December evening, John was driving on an icy rural road when he came upon a car in the ditch. A Good Samaritan, he stopped to offer assistance. As he stood there, another car, driven by a drunk driver, hit John's car, pushed it into the stranded car, and crushed John's knee between them.

John was airlifted to a local hospital for emergency surgery. As he awoke from the anesthesia, he became aware that his estranged brother, Carl, was standing beside his bed. He felt Carl holding his hand and heard him repeating, "I love you."

The tragic event renewed their relationship. Eventually the family reconciled, the two companies merged, and the family business, as well as the family, was healed and whole. Love—expressed, demonstrated, initiated—started strengthening family bonds that overcame past hurts and misunderstandings.

Statistics of Love

Family businesses comprise 80 to 90 percent of enterprises in North America.[ii] Yet operating a business as a family is no easy task—personalities add an extra level of pressure and potential conflict. This is statistically evident when you remember that less than one-third of families control their business into the second generation, and only about one in ten are still viable into the third generation.[iii] That's why it's so important not to take love for granted.

Based on my experience, the largest obstacle to family business succession planning is poorly expressed appreciation, recognition, and love. This blind spot crosses genders, generations, and ages. Working with family business clients, I have talked with owner-entrepreneurs who desperately want to know whether what they have done—creating and maintaining a successful business—is recognized as making a difference. They want to know that their families love them.

Of course, adult children love their parents, right? There's the rub—many take their parents for granted and fail to tell them they love them or appreciate the business platform that's been built.

Across generations I've often heard, "Oh, they know I love them." Or, "It's obvious, I don't have to talk about it all the time." I usually reply, "Of course you love them, but let them know it, too."

Strengthening the love in your family helps the bottom line. Here are three simple ways you can strengthen your family and your business:

1. Regularly and genuinely tell your family that you love and appreciate them and what they mean to you.
2. Spend time individually with other generations outside of the business to build the emotional equity of your relationship. Get involved with one another's lives.
3. Actively engage one another through family meetings to share your family values on money and wealth, and help develop purposeful lives through stewardship and service.

Create every opportunity possible to build the emotional equity of your family, even as you build the equity of your company. It costs nothing, takes very little time, and it works.

Formalizing the Love

> . . . He will not go behind his father's saying,
> And he likes having thought of it so well
> He says again, "Good fences make good neighbors."
> Robert Frost, "Mending Wall" (1914)

Although poet Robert Frost's proverb, "Good fences make good neighbors," rings true for neighbors, when it comes to family business, I suggest a variation: "Formal structure supports family love." Having a structure and shared vision can prevent family rifts from undermining a thriving enterprise.

Yet it's not unusual for family businesses to put off dealing with issues as a way to maintain family unity. Of course, what happens when issues are not discussed and resolved is that more issues arise, and this inadvertently creates the very problem the family is trying to avoid.

Bottom line: Family businesses, like all start-ups, need structure to grow. In my experience, family members in business generally love and care about one another. They try to do what's best for their company and to avoid fights. Especially in start-up companies, each working family member operates independently, with little official structure or formal communication. This creates communication voids. Individuals make assumptions without a shared understanding, and small differences fester unresolved until they become painful and unmanageable.

If a family business is operating without a hand on the tiller, administrative decisions are being made by the bookkeeper without recognizing how they affect other parts of the company. Feelings are hurt; complaints become personal. That's typically when I am called in—when feelings are raw and people aren't talking.

Believe it or not, this is not unusual. I might even say such situations can be expected in family businesses that run "on their own." Business and family issues overlap without oversight, and family entanglements upset business functions. Even normal business and financial differences can erode family relationships. That's because two separate systems—family and business—have become intertwined. Business activities erode family relationships, and family relationships put stress on the business.

Find the Balance

Family-owned firms need to find, define, and develop the balance. This is necessary so that a business family can be both a business and a family without one overly influencing the other.

When there is too much overlap, the business is vulnerable to family issues and entangle-

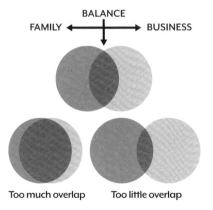

ments that are normal in all our families. In addition, business differences often harm family relationships.

On the other hand, when there is too little overlap, it robs the business of all the positive qualities of the family culture. It's these positive qualities that contribute to family businesses outperforming the financials of companies in the Standard & Poor's 500 index.[iv] Family businesses are the source of most new employment and are also a major contributor to the gross domestic product.

The way to create balance between the two systems is to have structure and formality—something that all family businesses need to create. Typically when I suggest this, the client's response is, "We don't need all that corporate stuff because we love one another." My response is always, "It's because you love one another that you need this stuff."

Start by Sharing

A family business needs three types of meetings to formalize expectations for the company:

1. **Family meetings.** These begin first so that the family can discuss the expectations and operations of the company and the family's approach to business. It is also a way to manage the boundary between business and family. Everyone in the family is invited to family meetings, even  those who may not be working in the company but are affected by its decisions. A lot can be accomplished in these meetings to bring understanding, healing, and power to individuals as well as the entire family. Family meetings are one of the ways to create structure, formality, and balance between the two systems.

Family meetings are also the place where family members formulate their expectations for the company and communicate them to the board of directors.

2.   **Business meetings.** These meetings are where the employees implement what the board has created in terms of the family's expectations for the business. Only company employees attend these meetings.

3.   **Shareholder and board meetings.** These meetings monitor and discuss the company's performance. This assumes that the company has specific, measurable processes and goals and that the board has real influence and governance. Only shareholders or board members attend these meetings.

As you can see, family meetings are at the heart of what continues within the business. They are the foundation for the core values that underlie the corporate culture of the family firm, as well as the management and governance of the business. Set out in Tables 1–3 on the following pages is a summary of what family meetings are all about. I encourage anyone involved in a family business to use this template as an opportunity to begin meaningful communications and to catch little irritations before they become big fights. Doing so will permit the family that controls the company to set its course, develop its strategies, and execute its plan on the most solid foundation possible.

The Hubler Checklist™: Family Meetings
TABLE 1: FUNCTIONS OF FAMILY MEETINGS

Creating balance between the family and business system
Opportunities to build the emotional equity of the company
Creating a Common Family Vision™ to unite the family
Shareholder education
Family unity
Celebration and renewal of family rituals
Transparency
Creation of a Family Participation Plan™ (family employment policy)
Creation of expectations for the performance of the company (return on investment)
Succession planning discussions
Communication
Estate planning discussions
Management of differences
Wealth preparation planning and philanthropy discussions

The Hubler Checklist™: Family Meetings
TABLE 2: BENEFITS OF FAMILY MEETINGS

Family harmony
As a family, living in gratitude
Business success
Identifying family values regarding wealth, philanthropy, and service
Transparency
Successful succession planning
Successful adult children
Having a strong sense of purpose

The Hubler Checklist™: Family Meetings
TABLE 3: FAMILY SKILLS

Talking skills (sharing)
Management of differences (problem solving)
Listening skills (understanding)
Forgiveness (reconciliation)

In 2008, a father and his son started Jones Construction. At that time, the Great Recession was challenging all businesses, especially construction. Yet, Jones Construction experienced wonderful financial success, growing from nothing to $7 million annually in 2012, with a $500,000 profit. On the outside, Jones Construction looked like a thriving business with remarkable prospects and a great future.

But inside the family was unhappy. In addition to the father and son, the father's wife (the son's stepmother) and the son's wife were also engaged in the business: The stepmother was the estimator, and the daughter-in-law was the bookkeeper. The two women weren't speaking to each other. This strained the relationship between the father and son, who had founded the company. They needed to do something to restore family relationships and maintain the company's success.

ADDRESS THE ISSUES

We began with an initial family meeting to find some common ground. We talked about the issues, concerns, and challenges that the business and family faced. In follow-up meetings, we developed an action plan to address the issues that were identified. Here are a few of them:

- Updating and producing a well-constructed buy-sell agreement
- Preparing a Common Family Vision™ to unite the family
- Developing a financial exit strategy
- Discussing and determining who will lead the company and who will produce a business plan
- Leveraging contributions to the 401(k) plan
- Getting everyone talking!

They had a lot of work to do. The family meetings started by creating the first-ever Jones Common Family Vision™. Each family member wrote his or her own individual vision and shared the family values most important to that person—so important that the family member wanted to see them perpetuated in the company. This helped balance the critical zone where family values and business requirements come together.

CREATE A FAMILY VISION

Discussed in more detail in the next chapter, an ideal Common Family Vision™ should unite the family around its shared values. Each family member should aspire to achieve his or her vision, realizing that no one will ever get one hundred percent of what they want. However, each person is called upon to make a contribution to the common good out of their generosity, love, sense of abundance, and the trust that "if I make a contribution now, other family members will do the same when their turn comes."

It's so important to do this that I encourage each member to recite the Common Family Vision™ every day. As both a promise and a rallying cry, it continually reinforces the reciprocal commitment that family members have made to one another's success in the team.

JONES COMMON FAMILY VISION™

The strength of our family business is our dedication to one another, our employees, and the quality of our work.

We create a legacy of integrity that is committed to acceptance, kindness, and respect for one another that allows us all to grow, have fun, and enjoy our work.

STRENGTHEN COMMUNICATION SKILLS

Once the Jones family had written its Common Family Vision™, they started having regular family meetings to strengthen the family's communication skills. I introduced them to Sherod Miller's Collaborative Team Skills[v] process to make it easier. Miller has devoted his professional life to effective communication. The program in its original format was titled "The Minnesota Couple Communication Program," and the business iteration became Collaborative Team Skills. Collaborative Team Skills is a practical, skill-building program about communication styles, talking skills, listening skills, and problem-solving skills.

The program begins by educating family members about the two aspects of communication, the what and the how. Of these two, the how (the style) can be more important. Each family member worked diligently to improve his or her communication—and it worked. Just learning how to share feelings made a huge difference in resolving issues. They learned to share hurt feelings instead of acting out the hurt. It may sound like a play on words, but in action it was a game changer for the family.

With improved communication skills, the family used its meetings to discuss expectations. All relationships are bilateral, which means one person needs the others to carry out their respective roles at work or in the family. It's the same idea as stardom: A movie star cannot be a star unless there's a supporting cast. This is true in all our relationships. In a movie, the cast knows what to say and do, but in life and work those actions are ambiguous or assumed. Yet each of us has expectations about what a good co-owner, spouse, sister-in-law, father, or son does. We need to discuss those expectations so that everyone knows. When the Jones family talked about expectations, everyone began to understand and respond, and things improved.

UNDERSTAND ONE ANOTHER'S WANTS

The father and his wife were able to share what they needed from each other to thrive. For instance, the father needed the space and time to do things the way he wanted rather than how his wife wanted. On the other side, the wife wanted to be heard and respected for her opinion.

The stepmother and daughter-in-law worked hard to learn how to negotiate their expectations. They shared what they needed to thrive and learned how to make appropriate adjustments. For example, each of them agreed to check out her assumptions and give the other the benefit of the doubt before just assuming the other was trying to hurt her.

The father and son also learned to get comfortable sharing what they expected from each other in order to thrive, communicate respect, and show their love. I was honored to witness a moment when they renewed their commitment to each other. They continued on to comfortably work as a team to confront and resolve succession planning and other issues the company faced.

Here are a few examples to demonstrate how significantly the father and son brought things into balance:

- They hired an operations manager consultant to guide them in reorganizing the company. In that process they clarified their roles, developed a business plan, and are considering hiring a general manager to run the company.

- The father is working with a new company accountant to develop his financial exit strategy and determine how his son will acquire the father's half of the business.

- Both the father and son are working with their new company attorney to revise and update the buy–sell agreement.

- The father and son are working with their new 401(k) vendor to correct previous errors so that all recipients achieve maximum benefits.

MAKE RELATIONSHIP COMMITMENTS

Jones Construction is a small family business that made family meetings a pathway to a whole new sense of family and business. The family will hold two family meetings a year as a way to maintain progress. They tell me that every day they recite their Common Family Vision™ and reciprocal commitment to one another's success. They will use the communication skills they learned in the Collaborative Team Skills process to efficiently manage their differences.

Large or small, complex or simple, start-up or generational, in my opinion, business families enjoy life, family, relationships, and business much more when they take the time to formalize their love.

2

THE SOUL OF FAMILY BUSINESS

"When you do things from your soul,
you feel a river moving in you, a joy."
Jalaluddin Rumi

Family Values: Heart *and* Soul

A family's history and values are central to the firm, whether you realize it or not. The heart and soul of a family business are its values,
which underlie the corporate culture of the enterprise and create the
essence of a family business' unique competitive strengths. It is the
"secret sauce" element that distinguishes it from competitors and
can make it a special place to work.

In my many decades of working with family businesses, I have
learned that these values emerge from multiple sources. The sources
include family history, religious values, hardship and adversity, and
the value of hard work and determination. This chapter will focus on
how all the stakeholders of a family-controlled business enterprise
identify and nurture the values that are so essential to family business success.

These elements are critical to fostering soul in family business:

- The emergence of shared family values

- The creation and nurturing of a Common Family Vision™ based on family values, and the development of the family's emotional equity

- Family kything (more on that on page 31) and a reciprocal commitment to one another's success

- Introduction of a model for collaborative communication

- Regular and periodic family meetings to promote family dialogue and values

- Solidification of the moral infrastructure

- Ethical norms based on family values

Perhaps the most perplexing question in the context of family businesses has to do with the nature of a family's "soul." From my perspective, this soul is what drives all of what happens in family businesses, and it is the indefinable essence of a family's spirit, being, and values. It is an issue that can and should be of profound importance to the largest and the smallest of family controlled enterprises. Here is what William Clay Ford Jr., chairman of Ford Motor Company, said on the subject in *The New York Times*:

> *I don't know if a company can have a soul, but I like to think it can. And if it can, I'd like our soul to be an old soul—and everything that implies. I'd like to talk about things like values and soul. These things aren't transient. These are things you build forever.*[i]

Soul is not something that can be measured or quantified, but it is easily recognizable by both its presence and absence. The soul of family business is not easily defined. I've gathered the following attempts to reflect its nature to give you a sense of the challenge.

David Whyte, in his book entitled *The Heart Aroused*[ii], quotes James Hillman and his definition of soul, saying: "Its meaning is best given by its context . . . words long associated with the soul amplify it further: mind, spirit, heart, life, warmth, humanness, personality, individuality, intentionality, essence, innermost purpose, emotional quality, virtue, morality, sin, wisdom, death." The soul, according to David Whyte, "has to be imagined as . . . given by God and thus, divine." The result: It is important for families to be vigilant and receptive when the soul comes knocking, with its implied sense of virtue and conscience.

It is important to understand that the soul will emerge, but you must be receptive, vigilant, and accommodating when the family's soul cautiously presents itself. The recognition of the soul is not an automatic process; it requires the family to quiet itself so as to be able to recognize the soul when it emerges. One of the primary ways in which a clinically trained advisor to family firms can intervene effectively is to assist the members of a business-controlling family to create enough quiet in the family for family members to recognize their soul when it presents itself. At the same time, managers of the family business can focus all their energies on enhancing business competitiveness.

Clearly, the family soul is shy, reticent, and easily spooked. At the same time, it is persevering and can be relentless with its message. What we need to understand is how to create an environment where the soul's message can be savored and brought into the presence of family consciousness. The soul's presence, according to Whyte, is "the palatable presence of some sacred otherness in our labors." It does not make any difference whether you call that otherness God, the universe, destiny, life, or love; for me it is the source of moral consciousness and creates the family point of view and family values.

The Primacy of Family Values

The manifestation of the soul in family business, from my perspective, emerges as a result of discussion of family values. These values are those that the family wants to see perpetuated in the company, and they serve as a rich source for family creativity, ethics, and moral stance. In my experience, and in the consultation process we use, the family is asked, "What are the family values that you would like to see perpetuated in the company?" As a result of this question, a rich family discussion can occur where family values are shared and prioritized. The discussion is often enlightening for family members as they begin to verbalize and connect emotionally in a conscious way around their common family values.

For me, these values are utilized in the creation of a Common Family Vision™, which I introduced in the Jones family case study. It becomes the moral compass for the family as it creates the ethical climate for its family business and the foundation for the evolution of the family point of view. This family point of view is the gyroscope that guides managers, directors, and owners as they build a corporate culture, develop corporate strategies, and execute their business plans.

Common Family Vision™

The tradition of making resolutions at the New Year dates back to the early Babylonian and Roman times, when promises were made to pay debts, return borrowed objects, and make resolutions to the god Janus. It's an opportunity to partake of the requisite tradition of making resolutions, where each of us resolves to challenge ourselves with self-improvement.

In the context of family businesses, creating a Common Family Vision™ is an alternate and more successful way of making a promise or resolution to contribute to the common good of the family. The Common Family Vision™ is created out of those values a family wants to see perpetuated in their business.

A well-crafted and heartfelt vision symbolizes the family's commitment to unite, create harmony, and improve communication. It also recognizes that no single family member is ever going to get one hundred percent of what he or she wants. At its very best, the vision inspires each family member to contribute to the family's common good out of their own generosity, love, sense of abundance, and the trust that if one of them makes a contribution now, another member of the family will do the same when their turn comes.

The Common Family Vision™ comes from the family's desire to unite the family around their values and, ultimately, their soulfulness. The Common Family Vision™, alongside uniting the family, also inspires family members to both collectively and individually be able to manifest the vision in all aspects of their work and personal lives.

For the Common Family Vision™ to have a significant impact on the evolution of the family's conscience and the creation of a family point of view, it needs to be something you nurture and reference on a daily basis. The benefits of a Common Family Vision™ and its value to the family may then be accomplished as a group or by an individual family member. The individual or family can measure their performance and whether they are behaving consistently with their Common Family Vision™. The daily recitation and repetitive nature embodies the spirit of the Common Family Vision™ and its values. The repetition is similar to that of high-performance athletes when their activities become second nature because of the multiple repetitions they perform. The same is true in families when they recite the Common Family Vision™ so that it becomes an embodiment of their soul.

The Common Family Vision™ also acts as an inspiration to help families achieve the goals that they are working toward—the idea is that they embrace the current reality and look to the vision. The energy that is created allows them to proceed toward the achievement of their goals, i.e., vision.

From a change perspective, the Common Family Vision™ allows family businesses to focus on the positive rather than the negative. The goal of the change process is to focus on the answer. One of the quotes that underlies this philosophy of the Common Family Vision™ is on the following page:

When I focus on what's good today, I have a good day.
When I focus on what's bad, I have a bad day.
If I focus on the problem, the problem increases.
If I focus on the answer, the answer increases.

I saw this quote hanging on the wall of a prospective Wisconsin-based family business client, and it was cited to "B.B., p. 451." It took me three weeks to figure out that it was citing the *Big Book* of Alcoholics Anonymous.

One example of a family that came together around a Common Family Vision™ is the Sweeney family. This family of two parents and four adult children owned a family business together, yet only the father and the oldest son worked in the business. The son and his father were having difficulties with the son's emerging role as a leader. In addition, the parents were concerned that the financial blessings that were coming to their adult children would have a negative impact on them and possibly, their grandchildren. The Sweeney Common Family Vision™ is thus:

> *Our family circle is an unbreakable bond of support, belief in one another, and unconditional love. It inspires us to live our lives with humility, integrity, and philanthropy. We manifest this through our families, our foundation, and our business.*

Again, the soulfulness of the family emerges in their Common Family Vision™ and becomes an inspiration to them as to how to lead their lives as a family, as well as their business and community involvement.

Prayer for Loving-Kindness

Another aspect of the Common Family Vision™ and building the emotional equity of the family is the prayer for loving-kindness. This is a ritual that we create for families, which includes the recitation of the Common Family Vision™, as well as the family prayer for loving-kindness. The prayer is:

May our family be filled with loving-kindness
May our family be well
May our family be peaceful and at ease
May our family be happy.

The goal of the prayer for loving-kindness is for participants to program their subconscious about what they want. The idea is to recite the prayer on a daily basis so that it becomes a continuum or embodiment of the family's soulfulness and virtues. It becomes an inspiration to use the Common Family Vision™ as a resource to unite the family.

Families are always trying to create unity within their families. The traditional methods for creating unity include compromise and giving things up; in contrast, I encourage you to set aside these notions and to understand that no individual in a family is always going to get everything he or she wants. Instead, family members should focus on doing what they can to contribute to the common good. A family member's understanding that they are furthering the common good makes it easier for them to make a contribution, as opposed to compromising and giving things up.

Serving the B.O.S.S.

Another facet of the Common Family Vision™ that supports the development and nurturing of soul in family business is the concept of B.O.S.S. The concept was developed by Sherod Miller[iii] in a communication and management-of-differences program that assists families in business to create a dialogue that allows their family point of view to emerge.

- **B** stands for — What does the **Business** need in order to be successful?
  The family needs to carefully consider the needs of the business in order to manage issues and prevent problems.

- **O** stands for — What do you want for the **Other** family members involved in the business regarding what they want?

  For me, the O is the most important part of the concept for family-owned businesses, where it is not unusual for family members to think that no one cares about what they want. Parents are prone to secretly hiding resentment and bitterness toward their adult children and to operate under the assumption that their children don't care about what they want. By the same token, adult children often mistakenly believe that their parents are not committed to their dreams of running a company. Only through a process of discovery, where family members share what they want for themselves and for the family as a whole, is each member of the family able to understand what the other family members want. This reciprocal commitment creates a team committed to one another's success.

- **S** stands for — What do you want for your **Self**?

  From my perspective, it is important to articulate what it is that you want for yourself—but a company can't survive based on only self-interest. It must be in the context of the greater Common Family Vision™.

- **S** stands for — What do you want for the other **Stakeholders**?

  This includes the family as a whole: the employees, the customers, the vendors, the board of directors, and sometimes the community.

The goal of the B.O.S.S. concept is to create win–win solutions that honor the Common Family Vision™ to help promote a common family point of view.

Another aspect of the creation of a cohesive team that allows for the emergence of soul is a synonym for the O part of B.O.S.S., which

Mihaly Csikszentmihalyi refers to as "psychic energy." He develops the concept of the autotelic personality, which he subsequently titled "flow." In his book, *Finding Flow*,[iv] Csikszentmihalyi investigates and develops an understanding about what gives people understanding in their lives. He indicates that there are three things that create meaning in people's lives: work, active leisure time, and relationships. When Csikszentmihalyi talks about relationships, he is referring to *family* relationships. And he is not talking about families of business or families of wealth, but rather he is referring to typical families and their need to build emotional equity. I believe that in families of business and families of wealth there is a greater risk of harm to the relationships because, as I've mentioned before, business and financial differences often erode family relationships.

What Csikszentmihalyi had to say supports the notion of reciprocal commitment to one another's success, which is also the O part of B.O.S.S. In *Finding Flow* he said: "A group of people is kept together by two kinds of energy: material energy provided by food, warmth, physical care and money; and the psychic energy of people investing attention in each other's goals." Essentially, Csikszentmihalyi states that it is critical to invest in the emotional equity of the family by paying attention to one another's goals and investing psychic energy into the family. At the same time, he says: "Now that the integrity of the family has become a matter of personal choice, it cannot survive except for the regular infusion of psychic energy."

Finally, Csikszentmihalyi writes about the idea of a joint goal, or what I call a Common Family Vision™, when he says: "Only when there is harmony between the goals of participants, when everyone is investing psychic energy into a joint goal, does being together become enjoyable." Basically, psychic energy is just another way of understanding the reciprocal commitment to one another's success: When you put psychic energy into the development of relationships in family business, as well as the family as a whole, it promotes the common good and the emergence of a family point of view through the promotion and embodiment of the Common Family Vision™.

The third form of promotion of a reciprocal commitment has to do with the concept of kything, a term discussed by Gail Straub in her book, *Rhythm of Compassion*.[v] Kything is another synonym for psychic energy (and the O part in B.O.S.S.). Kything is a Scottish word that means "connecting at a spiritual level." Kything is not psychological; it is spiritual—to kyth is to present your soul to another. The idea is that kything happens through communion, the evolutionary step in making the communion conscious or purposeful.

If each family member has an individual vision, they become a vision-driven person as opposed to being problem-focused. The idea is to put your spiritual energy into the wellbeing of another. M. Scott Peck, in his book *The Road Less Travelled*,[vi] called this concept love. The idea is for each family member to recite on a daily basis his or her own individual vision for what he or she is committed to and trying to do in their lives—both in and out of the family business.

The Common Family Vision™ is the embodiment of the soul of the family business. As well as the prayer for loving-kindness, the individual vision and kything prepare the soil, and it is the preparation of the soil that allows the spiritual seeds—the family's soul—to emerge in the concept of dialogue and the formation of the family point of view.

Collaborative Team Skills

For dialogue to emerge, I encourage family members to develop their Collaborative Team Skills, which consist of four components: talking skills, listening skills, communication styles, and mapping an issue or using problem-solving skills. Families sometimes resist implementing these fundamental skills, but I can assure you that even the New York Yankees go to spring training every year to brush up on the fundamentals. The talking and listening skills and communication styles are easily understandable and become a rich resource for the family in its ongoing dialogue. This applies to both the family and the family business as they sort out various issues. The benefit of using Collaborative Team Skills is having the whole family on an even playing field—all having the same model for communication and dialogue, as well as the same ground rules that will guide them to an effective discussion of the issues. The approach is in a simple format that makes it easy to introduce to family businesses.

The Collaborative Team Skills approach not only supports the development of effective dialogue in the family business, but it also supports the cross-cultural notions of Angeles Arrien in *The Four-fold Way*.[vii] In her seminars about her book, Arrien discusses the three cross-cultural rules that allow families to avoid conflict. They include: say what you mean, do what you say, and say it is so when it is so.

When it comes to saying it is so when it is so (avoiding conflict), Arrien operates on the "rule of three." The first rule is to say it within 24 hours; then if that is not possible, within three days; and then within an absolute maximum of one week.

Basically, the Collaborative Team Skills approach enables you to have the kinds of dialogue necessary to support family values. The purpose of the rule of three is to not let issues linger—it is not unusual in the context of families and family businesses for family members to avoid talking about something because they are fearful that if they do, it will upset family relationships. In public presentations, I often refer to this dynamic as Hubler's Speck of Dust Theory™. The theory comes from the work of C.G. Jung. Jung wrote, "Neurosis is always a substitute for legitimate suffering." Because all humans like to avoid pain and the sting of disappointment in our relationships, we develop mechanisms that allow us to avoid—essentially pretend— the realities of our life.

The same is true with Hubler's Speck of Dust Theory™ (this will come up again later in Chapter 4 when we talk about managing conflict, etc.). Family members are reluctant to talk about a business or financial issue in their family business because if they do it might upset the family getting together for a holiday—i.e., Thanksgiving, Christmas, or Hanukkah. They anticipate that the discussion of differences will disrupt family harmony, so to avoid talking about them, they pretend. As a result, they create the very thing they are trying to avoid: an unhappy family. In some instances, the avoidance increases the problem and creates more pain than the original issue. Utilizing the rule of three makes it possible for family members to discuss issues in a timely and current fashion.

It is in the context of these discussions that the family point of view emerges and their unique family resources develop to create the leverage and business advantage that allow family businesses to be successful. It is the "secret sauce" I've mentioned before—the unique set of spiritual principles that formulate the family's edge and give them their specialness in a way that affects their performance in the marketplace. Family businesses that continue to develop their soulfulness and that are committed to the development of emotional equity can anticipate strong dialogue and family resources that will abundantly and positively affect their firm's performance.

▌ FROM THE CASE STUDY FILES:
▌ THE THOMAS FAMILY VISION

When the Thomas family had a serious dispute among family members over ownership of their car dealership, we were able to tap into the family's religious traditions and values to help them resolve their conflict.

In Judaism, the High Holidays of Rosh Hashanah and Yom Kippur and the days of repentance in between allow for reflection of individual behavior backed by tikkun olam, the Jewish concept of forgiveness—a process of healing and repair. Similarly, the Christian tradition of Lent and self-sacrifice also influences the concept of the New Year's resolution.

The family was composed of hardworking, salt-of-the-earth, humble and close-knit family members. Historically, the members had been unassuming, and money had never been an issue in the family. At the time I worked with the family, there were several siblings and spouses working in the business. The father, who founded the business, was no longer active and sold the business to his three sons—but he got poor legal advice and sold the business below market value. He also excluded his two daughters from the estate plan.

As a result of the sale, the brothers were taking a combined compensation of one million dollars per year from the business and distributions. Both daughters worked at the dealership, so they both knew the compensation and distributions their brothers received. You can imagine the tension and hurt feelings that occurred as a result.

By developing a Common Family Vision™, the family members were able to resolve their differences. Older brother Mark, who was president of the business, supported a Common Family Vision™ that reflected the common good of all family members. Mark, his siblings and their spouses recited their Common Family Vision™ on a daily basis.

Despite complicated legal and financial business issues that had surfaced previously, the family members engaged in an emotional healing process that occurred over about eight months. During that period, the Thomas family was guided by its Common Family Vision™, which was created based on the members' family values and charted a path to a more successful and profitable business. The family participated in regular family meetings throughout this time to discuss emotional concerns, reorganize the ownership plan to include the daughters, and heal and repair family relationships.

In the process, family members also renewed their love and commitment to one another. The company has gone on to become the most successful business of its type in its state, and the family members have never been closer. By working collaboratively to create a Common Family Vision™ and by reciting it daily, the Thomas family members are united—and their dealership has thrived.

In our family and business we promote respect, honesty, fairness, and encourage an environment that is loyal and unified. At the heart of our vision is our commitment to generosity, quality, and an appreciation of one another's gifts. As a hard-working and dedicated family, we communicate and celebrate our spirituality.

MARK'S INDIVIDUAL VISION

My family and I are blessed by God's abundance. I am nourished by giving back.

FROM THE CASE STUDY FILES: THE LINCOLN-SMITH FAMILY VISION

The Lincoln-Smiths are two families who own a family business in common. Recently, one of the sons sued the family, and, in the wake of the lawsuit, the rest of the family members came together to create a vision focused on a new beginning for the family and company. This vision has been an inspiration for both the senior generation and the younger generation in establishing a family council. In the example shown here, the individual vision is that of the wife of the chairman of the board, who is not active in the company. Her focus is on dreaming dreams and sharing with others as a process of fulfillment.

LINCOLN-SMITH COMMON FAMILY VISION™

Because we embrace the past, we are presented with an opportunity to create a new beginning in which our family stands united by these values:

- *Respect*
- *Compassion*
- *Trust*

- *Generosity*
- *Fairness*
- *Integrity*

Guided by these values we are committed to:
- *Open communication*
- *Support of family goals*
- *Creating opportunities for success both inside and outside the business; you are able to follow your passion*
- *Giving back to the community*

NORMA SMITH: INDIVIDUAL VISION

I am appreciated, honored, and encouraged to be me. By dreaming my dreams and trusting to share with others, I am always fulfilled.

LINCOLN-SMITH FAMILY KYTHING

May (president) experience himself as an effective individual who manages challenges and guides others to a successful completion of tasks.

May (daughter) experience herself as compassionate, respectful of herself and others, and fair in dealing with family and employees.

May (son) and the business serve as a magnet to help draw the family closer together by providing opportunities that include dividends, jobs, philanthropy, and physical meetings.

The Business of Gratitude

> *"The hardest arithmetic to master is that which enables us to count our blessings."*
> Eric Hoffer (1903–1983)

According to former Fortune 500 CEO-turned-author and poet James Autry: "Gratitude doesn't come naturally. We have to learn it." We are not born grateful. Before it can grow beyond the polite expression of "thank you," I believe each of us must make our own journey to gratitude. That destination is the emotional result of a spiritual—not simply a social—process, according to Autry in his book *Choosing Gratitude: Learning to Love the Life You Have.*[i]

While achieving a sense of gratitude is not difficult, it does require conscious attention.

Why is it so important to learn gratitude, not just voice it? Because at that level, it is a business asset. In my experience, the single most troubling obstacle in family-owned businesses is that appreciation, recognition, and love are so rarely expressed. I consider it the biggest obstacle to succession planning (see "The Ten Most Prevalent Obstacles of Family Business Succession Planning" in Chapter 5 of this book).

What's the lesson in all of this? Don't take anyone for granted. All generations share in this lack of appreciation and recognition. Adult children in a business family love their parents but take them for granted. They fail to express thankfulness for what their parents have done to help them be successful. Parents also take their adult children for granted by failing to express appreciation for their commitment to the family business. They have not realized that living in gratitude is a choice, and what Alexis de Tocqueville might call "habits of the heart." Living in gratitude becomes a way of life, as it became for me.

Before I reached my forties, I was far more absorbed by what I did not have than what I did have. I saw myself as average and seldom considered my blessings or personal gifts. I was fairly accomplished professionally; I was a successful family therapist, a founding director of the Gestalt Institute of the Twin Cities and a recognized Bush Leadership Fellow, and I was initiating my family business consultancy. Yet I was focused on the private losses in my life. My boyhood with two alcoholic parents. The loss of our two sons at birth. A fire that gutted our home in 1979. All this negative pressure led me to participate in the program Adult Children of Alcoholics, where I began to embrace and emotionally own the experiences of loss that made me who I am today.

I began to realize the blessings of those difficult experiences and was then able to start focusing on their positive influences and appreciating the two lovely children my wife and I adopted. I attended seminars, wrote an autobiographical paper, shared the losses in my life, began meditating (difficult for the extrovert that I am), and decided to write a poem or two. All of this, over many years, helped me understand and be grateful for the blessings in my life.

My poem "Coming to Life Through the Blessings of Loss" (1998) now represents to me that door opening when I "came to life" to celebrate, own my gifts, and move on.

> *Oh, Loss, Loss, Loss.*
> *Oh, how I lamented the loss those many years.*
> *My childhood, my innocence, my children, my house, my voice.*
> *The inner bitterness swept over my life, like a pall squelching the spirit of my life.*
> *It is the most unusual awakening the day that I accepted the gifts of my life.*
> *Let me give voice to my*
> *Passion*
> *Joy*
> *Love*
> *Hope*
> *Energy*
> *Optimism*
> *Let me celebrate and take unto myself all the fruits of my life.*

It expresses what is so well stated by English minister and author Matthew Henry (1662–1714): "Thanksgiving is good, but thanks-living is better."

Benefits of Gratitude

So, you may be saying to yourself: "Okay. I get it. Gratitude is important and I should be thankful and say so. Is that so hard?" In a word, I would say, "Yes."

The benefits of gratitude are obvious but unfortunately seldom achieved because gratitude is so infrequently expressed. "Please" and "thank you" taught from childhood become expressions, though not necessarily of appreciation. They are given and taken to be polite. When was the last time you looked someone in the eye, grabbed their shoulder or hand, and took an extra second when you thanked them? It almost feels embarrassing, right? Too much? Awkward?

Why? Perhaps because we agree with the need to appreciate others, we have not learned how to express gratitude authentically. We assume it rather than state it. We diminish rather than acknowledge it. We shower it on a newborn and never nurture it as a person grows up.

Yet timely expressions of gratitude, however brief, can do wonders for any family or family business relationship, or for any business, for that matter. Expressing gratitude strengthens esprit de corps in a business family. It draws generations together and builds devotion among siblings and their parents because they show respect and appreciation for one another's gifts. When consciously done, expressing gratitude is one of the easiest and simplest ways to build the equity of the company—and it also does wonders for building character.

Let Gratitude Guide the Way

The philosophy of gratitude can help family businesses and the advisors who serve them.

German theologian, philosopher, and mystic Meister Eckhart (c. 1258-1327) wrote, "If the only prayer you ever say in your whole life is 'thank you,' that would suffice." According to author Angeles Arrien: "Gratitude is a feeling that spontaneously emerges from within. However, it is not simply an emotional response; it is also a choice we make."[ix]

I have come to realize that gratitude arises from awareness, from conscious practice, and from truly recognizing the good in our lives. Arrien proposes four universal portals to experience gratitude. They are:

1. **Blessings** — recognizing the good in our lives
2. **Learnings** — accumulating our experiences of growth and change
3. **Mercies** — exhibiting kindness, compassion, and forgiveness
4. **Protections** — striving to safeguard ourselves and loved ones

These portals or pathways help one to recognize and express gratitude consciously. In his book *Thanks!*,[x] noted psychologist Robert Emmons, a leading scientific expert on gratitude research, notes that it is easy to lapse into a negative mindset: "Gratitude is the way the heart remembers kindnesses—cherished interactions with others, compassionate actions of strangers, surprise gifts, and everyday blessings."

This doesn't mean you have to become a spiritualist, contort yourself into a yoga position, or meditate for hours. But it does mean that we must put gratitude into practice and intentionally develop more grateful thoughts.

How? By making gratitude a conscious choice, not an occasional incident. I practice gratitude in my own life by:

- Being conscious of being thankful often, every day

- Living in the moment to be part of (not just watching) what's around me

- Looking for ways to help someone else or "pay it forward"

- Serving and giving of myself and my time

Living in gratitude adds tremendous benefit to our lives. It has been shown to enhance physical health by reducing stress and lowering anxiety. The old adage, "Laughter is the best medicine," turns out to be scientifically true!

Gratitude allows us to acknowledge our talents and gifts and to discover the purpose of our lives. In my own case (which is not unusual), gratitude helps provide the sense of purpose that supports or even causes a meaningful career.

Gratitude is a critical ingredient in strong relationships. In families, friendships, and working relationships, gratitude is the glue that holds people and groups together. Teamwork, in my opinion, is a non-sentimental expression of gratitude.

Gratitude strengthens character because it turns us from wishing for what we don't have to appreciating what we do have. We focus on values, not hungers. We live in harmony rather than distraction. In fact, I would argue that living in gratitude makes one happier, healthier, more attractive to others, more inventive, more effective, and more efficient in all aspects of our lives.

Within business families, gratitude is a secret ingredient that can raise a company above its competitors, beyond the routine, and through difficult times. It can be as easy as showing that you appreciate employees and working family members. But it must be practiced, not performed, meaning it must come from the heart and represent real gratitude, not just a placating "Atta boy" (though the occasional off-the-cuff, genuine response can be priceless!).

FROM THE CASE STUDY FILES: THE GRATITUDE OF GRATIAN

As I write this, I'm reminded of a wonderful client of mine who recently passed away. I'll call him Gratian, which is Latin for grateful. Gratian began to work in his family's business when he was quite young and just after his father had died. Gratian provided the leadership to help his uncles and brothers transform the company. Eventually Gratian bought out his relatives and transferred the business to his two adult children. Through all of these transitions there could have been chaos, disappointment, disagreement, and discord. Instead, because of Gratian's honesty, integrity, and loyalty—in short, his gratitude—the family never wavered, and the company never faltered.

But, in looking back, what I marvel at the most is that Gratian taught himself to be grateful. He "wasted" work time to meditate or pray. Each day, he took a break from his busy schedule for a personal moment in his office to count his blessings and appreciate his family. And that made all the difference.

In my own life, much of who I became can be attributed to the generosity of Bishop Gerald O'Keefe, a former bishop of the Cathedral of Saint Paul in Saint Paul, Minnesota. Bishop O'Keefe recognized that I was a struggling inner-city kid who needed financial help for my tuition at the University of Minnesota. He gave me that assistance and said, "You don't have to pay the money back, but if you are ever in a position to help someone, I hope you will do so." His generosity caused me to dedicate my life to serving and helping others. His influence produced my passion so that I continually recognize and live in gratitude. It was the bishop's gift to me, and one I consciously pay forward.

I encourage you to accrue your own gratitude inventory. Take a moment each day to individually thank in your mind the people you love and who love you: your spouse, your parents, your children, a great friend, a close work associate, a partner, a person who altered your life. These brief moments accumulate into a sense of gratitude that you will learn to express; it will grow and become as natural as breathing. It fills your life with thankfulness for what you have, unconcerned with what you don't have.

3

FAMILY BUSINESS BEST PRACTICES

"Happiness is having a large, loving, caring, close-knit family
—in another city."
George Burns (1896–1996)

Happy Families, Healthy Families

Research, as well as common sense, tells us family businesses perform better and are more profitable when the family is in harmony and family relationships are solid. With that in mind, it is beneficial to explore what harmony is.

In itself, the condition known as "happiness" is somewhat of a mystery. Happiness in a family may align around family values and a Common Family Vision™ that springs from those values. It's powerful stuff, but there is more to happiness than aligning values.

In his research on families, David Olson, Ph.D., specifies three characteristics that create healthy families: flexibility, togetherness, and communication. The structure below relates the first two, and good communication brings them together.

Dr. Olson's model suggests that happiness generally occurs when a family is flexible and balanced in its structure and togetherness. Happiness is implied within the encircled area. The goal is to avoid being too flexible on the low end or too rigidly structured on the high end. The middle position allows the family to adapt to changes. Similarly, on the horizontal scale, having too little or too much togetherness can create a problem. Balance lies in the center of this diagram—but not necessarily in the direct center.

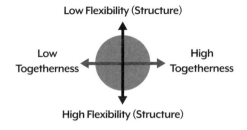

Source: David Olson, Ph.D.

For instance, if your children are young, you might want to structure the family's flexibility and togetherness toward the lower right portion of the circle. This attitude offers more structure (more consistency) and more togetherness (which helps a child feel safe). On the other hand, when children are teenagers or emancipated adults, the family's happiness is best represented by the upper left portion of the circle, with more flexibility and less need for togetherness—giving older children greater independence. The diagram also indicates that the further you move away from the center area, the more likely you are to find unhappiness in your family.

Good communication is the third characteristic of happy families. The most important communication skill is listening. Listening permits understanding, which is essential to happy families. Whenever you share your perspective, you should try to speak from the heart. Make "I" statements to help others understand your concerns. "I" statements help people speak for themselves and not for others.

Having a common approach to effective communication not only strengthens the family, but it also helps family members refrain from emotional disconnection both at home and at the office. This is certainly critical for a family, and it's even more important to the success and profitability of a business, according to the research of Dr. Olson.

Happy Families Lead Healthy Businesses

A healthy family is good for the family members and good for the business. In fact, the health of a family can be measured by the bottom line of its family business. Here are some characteristics that make up a healthy family:

Fun

Having fun as a family is often overlooked as a vital ingredient of successful families. Fun can be one of the first things to go when business tensions enter family relationships. Fun is important for its own sake. It relieves stress and tension, and it also builds and maintains the family's emotional cohesiveness. Fun does not require spending lots of money. Family gatherings, picnics, outdoor activities, walks, board games, reading together, and visits to local museums are all inexpensive activities that can lead to family fun.

Celebrating rituals

Family rituals are important for healthy families. Every family has them—bedtime routines, seasonal events, and religious ceremonies, for example. A family's rituals are the glue that binds them together. The family benefits enormously by celebrating them. Updating or creating new rituals that reflect the current growth and evolution of the family are also beneficial.

I have come across many special family rituals in my work:

- Family members eat a Christmas pudding in which a single hazelnut is hidden, and the person who finds it gets a special gift.

- Family members get to eat from a special plate on their birthdays.

- Families bond through annual hunting/fishing trips or family vacations.

- A father takes his teenage daughter on a 300-mile bike ride each year to raise money for the National Multiple Sclerosis Society.

- A family gathers with close friends to celebrate Independence Day every year by sponsoring a picnic to support a local nonprofit that serves inner city youth initiatives.

Common Family Vision™

A Common Family Vision™, as discussed earlier, is another key to a happier, healthier family.

A family I work with crafted a Common Family Vision™ that states: *Our family circle is an unbreakable bond of support, belief in one another, and unconditional love. It inspires us to live our lives with humility, integrity, and philanthropy. We manifest this through our families, our foundation, and our businesses.*

With that thought, this family has crafted a vision that unites them while doing good for their employees and the world. Each family member, at one time or another, will be called to contribute to the common good out of his or her generosity, love, sense of abundance, and most importantly, trust.

Praise

All too often, praise is overlooked in family life. Family members sometimes assume because they love one another, praise is unnecessary. I suggest the opposite: *Because* you love one another, it is important to regularly recognize and express appreciation to your family members for being special.

I have noticed that often the senior generation in a family business wants this appreciation and praise from their adult children, even though they may deny that they need or care about it. But deep down, they want to know their adult children appreciate their hard work and many sacrifices. That is also precisely what the younger generation wants. They want to be recognized and appreciated for their contributions and commitment to the family business. A healthy family is one where each member regularly gives and receives praise.

Beyond the key characteristics I've mentioned—fun, celebrating rituals, Common Family Vision™, and praise—there are others that develop a feeling of community. These include:

- Emotional support (being emotionally present)

- Esteem support (specific and exact praise)

- Networking support (belonging)

- Appraisal support (honest feedback)

- Altruistic support (giving to other people)

Being supportive is central to a healthy family. Nothing else in our culture can create the support that families offer. Healthy families regularly demonstrate these healthy behaviors in an environment that encourages and sustains them.

There is no one model for happy families. But it is most important to recognize that happy families are crucial to family business success. As you continue to build your business and your wealth portfolio, remember a healthy family is vital to it. Your family, like your business, needs specific and purposeful attention. At future family meetings, brainstorm ideas that nurture family fun. Look to create new family rituals. Share expectations with one another on how you want to be supported. Doing so will produce big rewards in your family, not to mention likely increases to the bottom line.

Mindfulness and the Management of Family Business Stress

If you are worried about stress—STOP. That only makes it worse. Stress causes deterioration in everything from your heart to your immune system. Good stress can be as draining as bad stress. Stress kills brains cells, and failing to manage stress can kill you.

Family businesses are fraught with opportunities for stress, including:

- Death of the entrepreneur/owner

- Business decline

- Management turmoil

- Firing of a family member

- Avoiding the discussion of critical issues for either the family or the business

- Erosion of family rituals as a result of business differences (e.g., family holidays)

- Impact of wealth and entitlement on the next generation

This is just the beginning of a long list of stressful situations that are a part of being involved in a family business.

When you have a family business, work and life stresses can have a profound impact on you. In my practice, I help family businesses learn to balance business and family obligations by keeping certain aspects separate, learning to communicate authentically, and setting goals together. Even in difficult situations, business families have drawn new boundaries and overcome rough circumstances to survive hard times and to thrive as both a business and a family.

In his book *150 Low Stress Jobs*, Laurence Shatkin[i] reports that workplace stress costs American businesses between $50 billion and $150 billion annually in worker health issues and lost productivity. Thus, stress carries high financial, physical, and psychological costs that can be doubly punishing in a family business.

What many consider normal day-to-day family issues can produce stress that can cause serious harm if unacknowledged. The following examples illustrate this.

Larry was the patriarch of the Mattison family business, SENTO. He recruited his son-in-law, Tim, into the family business, telling him, "I would like you take over my job." Tim left a successful position with a Fortune 500 company, thinking he would be the next president of SENTO. Years went by, and Tim still was not promoted to the top spot. Larry defended his decision by saying, "All I meant was that I wanted Tim to take responsibility for my sales account." Jen (Larry's daughter and Tim's wife) was upset with her father for the confusion he created and how he mistreated Tim.

In addition, Larry was struggling to let go of power, create a management succession plan, and develop a financial exit strategy for himself and his wife. This raised Larry's stress level, adding to the negative impact he had on family relations. Some would call these situations simply misunderstandings or issues that should be readily resolved—maybe so. But because of Larry, everyone in the Mattison family suffered under the stress.

FROM THE CASE STUDY FILES:
THE STEPHENS FAMILY

To save taxes, John, the owner of the Stephens family business, was told by his financial advisor to transfer two-thousand shares of stock into a family limited partnership with his three adult children: Ron, the oldest; Jerry, the middle child; and Philip, the youngest. The idea was that the three sons would eventually receive the value of the company in stock. John was the general partner and held voting control of the company, while the sons were limited partners in the venture. John found the stock transfer experience enormously stressful. Then things got worse.

Jerry and Philip worked in the business, and Ron had his own career. Jerry was the company's general manager, and he had recently fired

Philip, his younger brother. Jerry had different expectations of Philip's role in the company.

Philip had helped the company succeed until he was fired, and he resented his older brothers and father. He felt they ignored him and treated him unfairly. Philip also questioned Jerry's lifestyle and the compensation he received from the business. Additionally, he felt that Ron was abusing his position as a family member by running personal items through the accounting department. All of these actions contributed to a breakdown in communication and piled massive stress on the family.

As you can see from these examples, stress can produce deep divides. Stress can come from inside as well as outside. Our attitudes or perceptions may produce a stressful view of the world. You may have unrealistic expectations or live with fear, uncertainty, perfectionism, or low self esteem. But, few people can lower their stress until they recognize their own triggers.

Look at this brief list developed by Minnesota's Mayo Clinic. Are you experiencing any of these stresses in your family business?

- I'm impatient with details
- I make things happen
- I think most people seem to work too slowly
- I work long hours
- I have tight deadlines
- I need to talk in front of colleagues
- I have a lot of responsibility
- I work based on efficiency and vision
- I am hard on myself when I make a mistake
- I have been told I "have a lot of energy"
- I have overcome many hardships

These are all symptoms of stress and burnout, and by now this book itself may be stressing you out. Let's take a look at how mindfulness can help you manage stress in your family business.

When your brain perceives you are under threat, your body's stress response kicks in. These perceptions of threat don't have to be an encounter with a mugger or fear of losing your job. Subjective situations of almost any nature can trigger stress whenever the brain senses an imbalance of resources. Anything can cause you and your family business to feel stress: lack of control, lack of meaning in life or work, fear of the unknown. Stress is the friction between actual events and how one subjectively perceives them.

Sometimes circumstances can't be changed, but we must learn to control our perceptions of and responses to stressful situations. This resilience is not simply an ability to bounce back, but a conscious technique called Stress Management and Resiliency Training (SMART), developed by Amit Sood[ii], a Mayo Clinic professor of medicine. First, let's look at how our brains process stress.

How the brain processes stress

According to Sood, our brains operate in two functional modes: focused and default.

- In focused mode, we react to novel occurrences with an undistracted presence (i.e., "in the moment"). It could be fight or flight, pleasurable, meaningful, or some immediate experience in the external world.

- In default mode, the brain wanders and creates manifestations of the external world. This is the inner focus of our thoughts and reflections. Excessive internalization can create stress, anxiety, depression, and even attention deficit disorder.

The mind focuses on three primary aspects: threat, pleasure, and novelty. In the modern world, it might surprise you that threat is the primary focus, even though threat exists most often only in the mind.

But it is manifested by hurts and regrets of the past, as well as desires and fears for the future. Dr. Sood says this brooding creates "attention black holes" in the mind that take away the experience of joy and reduce bodily energy.

To combat the attention black holes, he proposes that we use SMART techniques to direct our attention outward—to others—where we can experience joy, happiness, and fulfillment.

How to employ stress management and resiliency training

It's likely too simple to say that SMART is a state of mind, yet it essentially is. To perform this Stress Management and Resiliency Training, Dr. Sood suggests three actions:

- **Joyful attention.** Begin each day, even before you get out of bed, by expressing gratitude for the special people in your life, such as your spouse, children, parents, friends, etc. From that early moment, be conscious so that when you return home from work you treat your family as if you are meeting them after a long absence.

- **Kind attention.** Practice caring and being kind—either directly or indirectly—to the first twenty or thirty people you encounter each day. You can express this attention silently with a kind look or verbally with a kind word.

- **Self-monitored intention.** Become aware of how you interpret events and activities as they occur. Recognize that you are viewing these through your normal lens, created by family and society, which prejudices and constrains your interpretations and causes stress. Instead, begin viewing life through the lenses of compassion, acceptance, acknowledging a higher power, forgiveness, and gratitude.

It's important to understand how forgiveness, compassion, and gratitude, which are the three most significant lenses, can alter your perceptions about what occurs in your family-owned business.

To BOD or Not to BOD

As a consultant to business families, I'm often asked, "Do you really need a board of directors?" My answer is always, "Yes and no."

Corporations are legally required to have a board of directors, but many entrepreneurial companies have a board meeting once a year just to satisfy the legal requirements. Essentially, those boards are inactive. So, yes there's a board, but no, it isn't made useful.

In fact, for entrepreneurs in family businesses, the idea of a board of directors is often seen as unnecessary or even onerous. When the entrepreneur is doing everything, the BOD just gets in the way. Even if a board might add value, it seems like an added burden or waste of time. Here again, the BOD is not allowed to be useful.

However, my answer to having a board is always "yes" when the business has multiple family members as employees and owners. Board and governance functions are on the business side of the equation, but an active board with outside advisory members adds value and often creates unity in the family. This becomes especially apparent when the originating entrepreneur needs to pass the baton to the next generation.

At some point the business in a family must be passed on if the business is to outlive the entrepreneur, yet I frequently tell entrepreneurs that they are irreplaceable. This would imply conflicting purposes, but it truly means you have to create a new system to replace the entrepreneur. The original entrepreneur must change his or her job description and become the architect and designer of the new ownership and governance system.

The new system should include an active board of directors made up of elected family members and independent outside advisors. A good process is to start with an advisory board and, if appropriate, eventually move to a legal board.

FROM THE CASE STUDY FILES: PETERSON REALTY

Everett Peterson was in the second generation of his family's real estate business. Initially, when his father died, Everett was in business with his uncles and brother, but over the years he bought out all of the other members of his family until he became the sole owner. He continued to grow the company into a highly regarded enterprise.

When Everett was in his early sixties, he recruited his son, Henry, to join the business. Everett promised Henry the opportunity to try new things to grow the business, but when Everett was struck with some serious health concerns, his tolerance for risk diminished.

When I first met Everett and Henry, their main concern was their father-son relationship, but after a few meetings with them, I clearly saw that their relationship concern was masking a larger issue related to business plans.

To begin, we wrote a business plan for Peterson Realty. I encouraged them to collaborate so that both Everett and Henry could blend their ideas about how to expand the company.

The more challenging solution was to create an active board of directors that included outside advisory members. Everett was reluctant to do this, but after a year of periodic discussions (yes, these decisions can take time), he saw its value and began to work with me to implement a board.

The first step was to create a prospectus. It was used to inform potential board candidates about the company and outline the board member's job description. Everett was skeptical at first about the caliber of the candidates he could recruit to join his board, but he was pleasantly surprised by the quality and professionalism of four outsiders that he and his son selected.

```
┌─────────────────────────────────────────────────┐
│                                                   │
│           PETERSON REALTY PROSPECTUS              │
│                                                   │
│          (Conceived by Everett with my support    │
│            and input from his son, Henry)         │
│                                                   │
│   ·   Summary of the Company History              │
│                                                   │
│   ·   Current Status of the Business              │
│                                                   │
│   ·   Current Business Challenges                 │
│                                                   │
│   ·   Owner's Goals                               │
│                                                   │
│   ·   Reason for the Board                        │
│                                                   │
│   ·   Characteristics of Candidates               │
│                                                   │
│   ·   Potential Candidates                        │
│                                                   │
│   ·   Frequency of Board Meetings                 │
│                                                   │
│   ·   Expectations for Committee or Requirement   │
│       for Work in between Meetings                │
│                                                   │
│   ·   Compensation                                │
│                                                   │
│   ·   Errors & Omissions Insurance                │
│                                                   │
└─────────────────────────────────────────────────┘
```

There were several initial goals for creating the board:

- Help with management succession

- Grow the business

- Have Henry report to the board rather than to his father

The board had four outside advisory members, with backgrounds drawn from banking, finance, management and business, and commercial real estate. Four members of the Peterson family also joined the board, including Everett's wife, Laura, and his daughter, Diana.

Over the next three years with the BOD, Peterson Realty enjoyed positive growth, innovation, and a healthy restructuring. The family, as well as Everett and Henry's relationship, has never been healthier. In addition, the initial board members termed out and new members were recruited.

What began as a means to strengthen Everett and Henry's father-son relationship became a plan that demonstrates how entrepreneurial companies can benefit from a board of directors that includes outside advisory members.

The Powers That Be

Understanding the give and take of sovereignty in family business

Parenting never ends —at least the urges don't —whether your child is two or forty-two years old. Parents may continue to intervene to prevent problems, assuming the interventions are in the interest of their children or grandchildren, without considering their children's opinions. This can cross boundaries, create sovereignty issues, and hurt feelings.

Myla and Jon Kabat-Zinn address sovereignty when they discuss parental intentions in their book, *Everyday Blessings: The Inner Work of Mindful Parenting.*[iii] In their seventh of Seven Intentions they mention "honor[ing] my children's sovereignty, and my own." Until I read this, I had not considered sovereignty in relation to my own children, let alone in family-owned businesses. A light bulb went on.

I recalled an occasion in my practice when the son-in-law in a family-owned company complained that his in-laws were usurping his own parental authority. Without his consent, they were providing his children with trips and excursions—activities that he felt were only in the domain for he and his wife to provide. He was also concerned that spending every Sunday with his in-laws was eroding his family.

The situation of another client was similar. A son in a family-owned business complained that his parents, however well-intentioned, were usurping his parental authority. They organized family meetings and discussed topics at those meetings that he felt only he and his wife should share with their children.

I recalled the complaint of another son, active in his family's business, that his mother's holiday gift giving preempted him and his wife as parents. His mother bought their children tickets to holiday shows without checking first with them.

Then I remembered a grandmother privately sharing with me her goal to create a happy family experience for her grandchildren. She was defining her job description of a good grandmother without consulting her son and daughter-in-law about what "good grand-mothering" might be.

In each of these cases, adult children were expressing the need for sovereignty. What is most unfortunate in these instances is that potentially everyone's feelings could be hurt. This issue is complex.

The adult children's financial or business reporting relationships with their parents complicated their ability to set boundaries and express expectations. Understandably, the adult children were reluctant to say anything to their parents that might further complicate the problem. The adult children thought, "If I, as a family member, say something, it will upset my parents, so I'm better off keeping quiet."

Do you know when issues of sovereignty come up in your family business? Do you have in mind some ways to handle them?

In my opinion, the best approach is to set aside some quiet time to clear the air so that everyone can share their expectations of one another as a member of the family and the family business. I suggest you create win-win situations that honor the integrity and sovereignty of both the senior and younger generations and share your perspective. Also, let other members of the family know your boundaries and share your expectations without judgment, criticism, or blame.

How did the son-in-law and daughter create a win-win situation when every Sunday had been spent at her parents' home? They established a "his and hers Sunday." On her Sunday, they visited her parents. On his, he had the option to do something with just his wife and their children. They respectfully communicated this plan to her parents. The senior generation was pleased to oblige. They understood the need for their adult children to have balance within their family.

Flexibility and a willingness to accommodate one another are critical to most solutions. All family members need to generously contribute to the common good.

When sovereignty issues arise in your family business or within the family, don't wait for them to escalate into a problem or misunderstanding. Reach out. Gather the family or those involved to discuss the matter. Start out by seeking to understand what others think and feel. Listen before you share your own expectations. Holding respectful, open family meetings like this can do much to reduce stress and encourage strong family bonds that recognize sovereignty.

Don't Mix Business with Family Holidays

The holiday season is a time to build family values and enjoy family members—not a time to debate business strategy.

The music of the holiday season fills our lives. We have images of chestnuts roasting on an open fire and family gatherings to light the candles on Hanukkah—or at least that is the popular mythology we think about for the holidays.

But for members of family-owned businesses, the holidays can be a very different story.

For me, preparing for the holidays means viewing some of my favorite films. At the top of my list is *The Bishop's Wife*, a 1947 film starring Loretta Young, Cary Grant, and David Niven (it's been more recently remade starring Denzel Washington).

The film is a classic metaphor for an entrepreneur and family-owned businesses. The story is about a bishop (David Niven) and his wife (Loretta Young), who is involved in parish life. The bishop is driven to raise money for a new cathedral at the expense of everything else in his parish, including his family. In the midst of the holiday season and beleaguered by his responsibilities, he asks God for help to relieve the pressure. God sends him an angel (Cary Grant) who, through a series of tricks, helps the bishop realize that his real mission in life is not to build a cathedral but to serve the needs of his parishioners.

In family businesses, the entrepreneur often becomes focused on building a cathedral (the business) at the expense of his or her family relationships. At holiday gatherings, it's not unusual for business discussions to dominate the gathering. As a result, family members who are not active in the business may feel left out—as if the business was the family. In the film, the bishop is so focused on building the cathedral, he ignores his wife, and the angel becomes smitten with her.

But just as the bishop eventually realizes his real mission—to serve parishioners—it is also true that an entrepreneur's mission is to serve not only the business, but also to be the guardian and steward, along with his or her spouse, of family traditions and rituals. It's these family and holiday rituals that bind the family together and create the richness in families that make holidays so lasting and special, and ultimately contribute to the wellbeing of the family business.

Whatever your traditions, the holiday season is a wonderful opportunity to set aside the stress and strains of the business and celebrate all the special family moments. As we gather to celebrate the holidays, we build the emotional value of family. This not only strengthens our families, but it also continues to inspire and strengthen each family's values. The celebrations help imbue the company with those values, which are the foundational core of the family's business culture.

During the next holiday season, seek new and innovative ways to celebrate that are inclusive and family-oriented. Form a family holiday committee to evaluate if what you are doing to celebrate as a family is working. If it is, keep it; if not, create a new approach. Put the family in charge, and keep it there. And remember: Keep normal business discussions in the boardroom and out of holiday gatherings.

Here are some ways to strengthen your holiday celebrations:

Be clear with one another about your expectations for the holidays
Spend time talking with one another before the holidays arrive to make sure you all understand what you want to get out of the holiday season.

Do your best to focus your time and energy on activities that celebrate family traditions and the blessings of the holiday season.

In those instances where you've outgrown family traditions or the family has become too large to reasonably continue the tradition, create new ones that allow you to experience the joy and love of your family.

Do your best to limit business discussions. Save them for the boardroom or for a regularly scheduled family meeting
Sitting around the table on Christmas Eve or the first night of Hanukkah is not the appropriate forum for airing business activities, successes, or problems.

Finally, and most of all, have fun
It's important to have fun with one another and connect or reconnect with those family members you often don't see. In the event you see your family regularly at work, go out of your way to renew, rekindle, and enjoy a side of your relatives you would otherwise not experience.

The holiday season provides a great opportunity to emphasize the family values that are the bedrock of your family. As you plan family activities, understand that less is more. Consider what you can do to create balance and harmony, and enjoy the family and the life you've created.

Separating Business from Family

"It's just business."

This comment is made on a regular basis in the world of business. It is so commonplace that we even hear it when dealing with friends and family on a transactional level.

It means decisions made in business are not to be taken personally. Business decisions may be harsh and hurtful; however, when it is "just business," these decisions are not a reflection of either party on a personal level. How do you keep that mantra true in a family business, especially when the person being reprimanded, placed on leave, or even fired, is a blood or legal relative? The good news is, it is possible. The bad news, of course, is that it is not always easy.

Set clear boundaries

Family business is never easy. Personalities that often butt heads are expected to work together for a common good. While that can be easier to do when the parties involved can go home at the end of the day, families do not have that option. After a fight at the office or a difference of opinion, the members of family businesses must still see one another at dinner or the next family gathering.

One way to help make the transition from work to home smoother for a family business is setting clear and visible boundaries. The most successful family businesses have clearly defined rules for business versus family time. For instance, family members may not be permitted to discuss business issues unless they are in the office, whether it is a home office or an external place of business. Additionally, they may not be permitted to bring any work into their home or family gatherings. These are just two simple examples of boundaries. Other boundaries may be much more defined or even complex, depending on the type of business and the family members involved.

Make time for family

Making time for business is inevitable. We all have bills to pay and items we want, and it all costs money. Therefore, we are ingrained to make time for work. At the same time, we are constantly told to make time for ourselves; however, when you own or work in a family business, you forget the importance of making time for family.

Family surrounds you in the office or on the job daily, so you may feel as though you already have made time for family. Yet in reality, all you have done is made time for work, which happens to include family. Making time for family means doing things with your family that remind you of how precious they truly are to you and your personal happiness. This philosophy will help your family survive the family business both at home and at work, allowing business to truly be "just business."

Coming Into Money

Family discussions about wealth are like family discussions concerning sex education: They are often avoided. During a recent consultation with a prominent client family—beneficiaries of a very large estate—I asked them how they were preventing their children from becoming spoiled. Despite their concerns and solid family values, they were stymied. They had not done anything to prepare their children for the wealth they would inherit.

On another occasion, I asked a client if she had discussed the family's wealth with her children (two were in college and the third was about to enter). "No," she said. "I don't want them to find out because if they do, I'm afraid they will lose their incentive to work and be productive." She planned to wait until they were older. Her response is not unusual.

How do families blessed with enormous financial success raise children who are not spoiled by it? Avoiding talking about it is likely not the solution. In fact, when we interview the children in preparation for a family discussion on wealth, they usually already have some clue about the family's status by virtue of their lifestyle, such as cabins and luxurious vacations.

Wealth creates issues just as a lack of wealth does. The question is, which set of issues do you confront? Sharing with your children that the family is blessed financially can set in motion a lot of possibilities. But the good news is that by telling them earlier, you have time to positively influence and guide your children. If you wait and spring it on them when they are older, you could set in motion a different set of possibilities for which you have not yet had the opportunity to prepare them.

In my practice, I have found that holding intergenerational family discussions is a wonderful opportunity to guide, inform, and prepare children for their stewardship responsibility. I believe if they are gradually and adequately prepared, children come to understand the meaning of their wealth and what role money will play in their lives.

These family discussions, which we call Wealth Preparation Planning™, begin when parents take the initiative to bring the family together and organize an agenda to talk about wealth. As parents live out their values regarding money, they represent strong role models for their children. It is a matter of identifying those values and using them to inspire their children regarding future spending, investing, saving, or sharing the wealth handed down to them.

To set the table for discussion, we suggest that our client families address the topic of wealth by asking, "How do we define success?" This becomes an excellent framework for describing values.

Then the discussion can evolve to, "What strategies should be in place to accomplish our goals?" These strategies for success relate to many critical areas, including:

- Family
- Business

- Attitude of gratitude

- Purposeful living

- Happiness

- Philanthropy

- Service to others

- Financial education

- Next generation planning for grandchildren

- Values

- Legacy

- Positive financial habits

- Money mentors

This is a partial list that can produce lively discussions in families who have the courage to take on the task and explore the challenges associated with wealth. What matters is not the extent of your wealth, but your family, its values, and how you use that wealth.

Take a moment to ask yourself, "What do I want my legacy to be concerning wealth and our family?" Then take the next step. Initiate discussions within your family so that your wealth intentionally demonstrates your family values.

Five Secrets of Highly Successful Family-Owned Businesses

My mantra when working with clients is, "It's always easier to prevent a problem than to try to fix one." The best practices that I've discussed in depth in this chapter can be summarized in the following five secrets of highly successful family-owned businesses.

1. They minimize potential conflict with a board of directors.

No matter what kind of outside opinions you bring in, the goal of a board is to provide counsel that can lead to more objective decision-making. They also bring a wealth of experience and valuable perspective to your firm. The question is: How are you going to replace the entrepreneur? Many times, the founder of a family business is difficult to replace, for a number of reasons. An outside board can help with that process.

In many ways, the founder is irreplaceable, so you can't find another person to take his or her place. But you can come up with a system to help with the eventual transition, and the system is a board of directors with either outside advisors or outside members.

By having a board, the younger-generation adult children no longer report to their parent, which can immediately reduce potential conflict. The younger generation reporting to a board of directors resolves and/or minimizes some of the conflict that can go on between the senior generation and the younger generation in family business.

2. They embrace structure with regular family meetings.

As I've noted previously, there are three types of meetings you need to have in a family-owned business. You need to have shareholder and owner meetings, and only the shareholders, owners, and board members get to go to those meetings. You also need to have employee meetings for people who work at the firm.

The third type of meeting is the family meeting. The purpose of family meetings should be to help manage the boundary between the business and family relationships. Everybody should be invited to those meetings, including spouses and other siblings who may not be active in the business.

Part of what can happen in family-owned businesses is that there are two systems—the family system and the business system—and the overlap that can exist between the two systems can cause conflict. It's an organizational problem that people within family businesses experience as an interpersonal issue, and oftentimes the way they deal with it is to blame others. But balance can be found between these two systems by adding structure and formality, in particular by making sure to maintain these three types of meetings on a consistent basis.

Many families I work with first resist, thinking they don't need structure or formality since they are family. I say to them, "It's because you are family that you need structure and formality, and that's how you create balance."

3. *They create a Family Participation Plan™.*
One of the keys to success for family-owned firms is to establish a Family Participation Plan™ as soon as possible. A Family Participation Plan™ is a code of conduct for how you're going to be and how you're going to operate your family business.

Think of the plan as a set of ground rules that can benefit all of those involved. If you go to a ballgame, before the game starts, the umpires and the managers get together at home plate to go over the ground rules. The reason they do that is so they know what's going to be fair and what's going to be foul in terms of the ballgame.

Family-owned businesses start playing the ballgame of family business, if you will, and in some cases they start playing without a set of ground rules. Instead of figuring out the rules in the middle of the game, it's best to start with a set of ground rules to minimize opportunity for conflict.

Among other factors, a Family Participation Plan™ can include:

- The criteria for coming into the business

- What kind of education will be required (or encouraged)

- Expectations on whether you need to have outside work experience before joining the family business

- Other eligibilities for joining the business

- The training program expectations

- What happens if mistakes or failures occur

- Compensation plan

- Issues related to career planning

4. *They work on their communication and conflict management skills.*

Strengthening family communication takes work, but it's worth it. I recommend using a program similar to Sherod Miller's Collaborative Team Skills[iii], designed to help families successfully manage their differences.

Whatever program is used, ongoing training to teach people how to successfully manage their differences and express their feelings, wants, and actions can greatly help the family business in the long run.

5. *They create—and adapt—their family vision.*

Having a Common Family Vision™, supported by a Family Participation Plan™, is important for family-owned businesses. Successful firms are able to use the family's values to create a Common Family Vision™ that can unite them and help them to see and articulate their reciprocal commitment to one another, and one another's success.

Family members should be able to know that every day they are putting positive energy into the business and family. That's what creates a team—people committed to helping one another be successful.

Note: For a more detailed discussion of the roles and priorities of shareholders, directors, and officers, as well as areas of work in family-owned businesses, see pages 192 through 198 of the Appendix.

4

MANAGING CONFLICT

Family Business Problems:
Do Family and Business Meet or Collide?

These intersecting circles help explain the vast majority of family business problems. The way I see it, the overlap between family and business is an organizational problem, but people within the family business experience it as an interpersonal

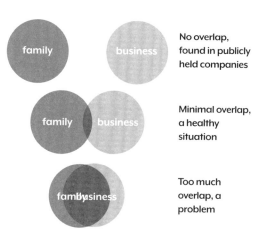

issue. That's why family members commonly blame one another for the situation. The senior generation sometimes blames the younger generation, and vice versa.

You then have to ask, "What causes the family business problem, and what's getting in the way?" It can be difficult to find the answer without the expertise and insight of outside advisors to help to resolve family disputes and avoid family litigation.

My approach is to simultaneously work on both the family and business sides of the equation to create a better sense of balance.

- Family — develop a Family Plan, outlining how to be a family without undue influence of the business.

- Business — develop Ownership, Management, and Leadership Plans, ensuring the continued success of the business, secure financial relationships, profitability, and positive family relationships.

Circles of Influence

One of the most common sources of conflict in family business occurs when people confuse their roles as owners and employees with those of being family members. Often there are unspoken, and conflicting, expectations on all fronts.

Two of my clients encountered this problem when family members employed as bookkeepers in the family business leveraged their status as owners and family members to trump business decisions—even when their position in the business didn't warrant such input.

It's also not unusual for the president of a family business to continue in that role when he or she comes home in the evening. The issuing of orders continues. One CEO client told his kids, "If you don't get a college degree, you're out of my will!" Not the best way to create family unity.

One of my favorite stories about conflicting expectations occurred when I was preparing to lead a seminar with the Minnesota Family Business Council. A father and family business leader called me to talk about a current concern. "I'm in business with my two sons; my oldest son is an engineer and my heir apparent," he explained. "He's been terrific up until two years ago when he got married. My daughter-in-law is the problem. Can you come and fix her?"

I quickly said, "I don't do that sort of thing." I didn't know what he was expecting, but it didn't sound very good to me. Instead, I suggested that he invite both his son and daughter-in-law to the seminar with other family members. He did.

Business and Family Circles

As I was presenting the concept of overlapping circles (where one circle represents the business and the other represents the family), the son raised his hand. "You know the way you've presented those circles—they're equal in size," he said. "If my dad were drawing those circles, his business circle would be very, very big. On the other hand, his family circle would be very small."

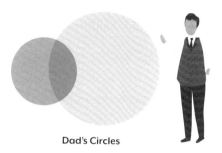

Dad's Circles

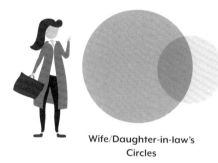

Wife/Daughter-in-law's Circles

"Now if my wife were drawing those circles, her family circle would be very big, and her business circle would be very small. So next time you do the presentation, I think you ought to mention that," he said.

Someone in the audience asked, "What do your circles look like?"

He bashfully said, "I'd rather not say." He was there with his whole family and caught in the middle between two people he really loved.

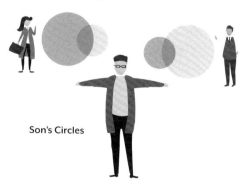

Son's Circles

After the seminar was over, the daughter-in-law came up and thanked me for suggesting that she be invited to the seminar. "Now I understand more about the culture of our family business," she said. "This is the first time as a family we've ever had an opportunity to sit down and talk about this. Thank you."

What this family did for the first time was discuss their expectations for one another and the business. You and your family also can discover the value of communicating about roles and expectations. I recommend that families sit down at a family meeting to discuss the following key questions:

> *What are our expectations for one another as family members?*
>
> *What are our expectations for one another as business owners/ employees?*
>
> *How can we best balance our roles as employees, owners, and family members?*

Clarifying and discussing these questions will go a long way toward creating family unity and eliminating unspoken expectations.

Forgiveness as an Intervention in Family-Owned Business

When family differences have broken or severed family relationships, is it possible to bring in your values and religious traditions to create healing? The answer is a resounding "yes!" But it must be done carefully. I use a Family Forgiveness Ritual™ paired with other family rituals as a tool to begin to focus on the future.

This ritual helps the family understand that hurts are inevitable in the context of family businesses, but that the ritual is a way to get beyond them and start over again. The Family Forgiveness Ritual™

draws on the family's history and use of religious traditions to create forgiveness and a new beginning.

In my original career as a family counselor, I worked in a medical clinic. My office was located in the specialty center right next door to the clinic where five family practice doctors regularly saw patients. It was not unusual in that setting for one of the nurses to come over and indicate that one of the doctors was seeing a patient and wanted to know if I was available to sit in on their discussion. Invariably, the patient was seeing the doctor for something for which the doctor could find no physical diagnosis.

I would then start seeing the patient for counseling, and usually what we discovered was a situation where the stress and discomfort in the patient's life was caused by some traumatic experience or wound. Someone, such as a parent, teacher, friend, or sibling, had hurt the patient, and he or she had not forgiven the person for what had been done. D. Patrick Miller, in his book *A Little Book of Forgiveness*,[i] mentions this dynamic in his own life and how it motivated him to write the book. He mentions that after multiple visits to his physician, he was referred to a psychiatrist who helped him realize the impact that not forgiving was having on his life. I learned at an early stage in my career the power of forgiveness, and much of the work I did in those days was helping people forgive the perpetrator of the wound so as to free the individual from continuing to relive the pain that they had experienced.

Fast-forward fifteen years—I found the same dynamics operating within family businesses. The assumptions, expectations, and role confusion that often plague family businesses can and do create major hurts in both family and business relationships that overlap one another and cause considerable hurt and frustration. It's not unusual in family businesses where this dynamic occurs for siblings, parents, and children not to be talking to one another or for various branches of the family to be excluding another branch. In some of the most dramatic cases, family members have sued one another. Witness the history of the Koch Refining family, as well as the Pritzker family situation, where one family member is suing another. In both these situations, people had not forgiven one another and then initiated the legal process as a remedy. The end result of the legal process will be to exacerbate the already strained family relationship to the point that a schism is created within the family that will affect the family for multiple generations to come.

The Family Forgiveness Ritual™ is designed to avert this process by ritualizing the process of forgiveness, drawing on the family's tradition of religious or spiritual values, and creating a ceremony that draws on the family's fundamental values of love, generosity, and sense of abundance. The goal of the Family Forgiveness Ritual™ is to bring the family's religious and spiritual traditions into its everyday life. Nash and McLennan discuss this very topic in their book on how to integrate people's faith lives with their lives at work, *Church on Sunday, Work on Monday*.[II] Their focus is primarily on public companies, so it seems this integrating should be much easier to implement in the context of a family business where all family members have a common religious or spiritual background.

Family Forgiveness Rituals™ are always done in the context of a family business consultation. The process starts with a series of individual interviews designed to create an understanding about the issues facing the family in preparation for the Family Business Planning Meeting. During both the individual interviews and the Family Business Planning Meeting, assessments are being made as to the family's readiness to achieve its goals. In those instances where obstacles to their achievement exist, family members are encouraged to use Collaborative Team Skills[iii] as a model to resolve their differences. To the extent they are not capable of being resolved in the family meeting context, it is not unusual to suggest either individual meetings or dyadic discussion to further explore how to resolve family business differences.

The introduction of the possibility of a Family Forgiveness Ritual™ is normally done in one of the early family meetings, but the details are specifically discussed in individual meetings. In these meetings, the concept of forgiveness and responsibility are broached and clients can discuss their response to the idea of participating in the ritual. It is important to note that Family Forgiveness Rituals™ are always done in the context of the overall consultation so that appropriate support and encouragement can be given before, during, and after the ritual has occurred. Family members are always encouraged to share their reservations as a part of the decision-making process as to whether or not to proceed.

One of the critical issues facing the consultant thinking about using the Family Forgiveness Ritual™ is the question of timing. In most instances, the ritual is used as a summary process to celebrate what the family has achieved through its family meetings and individual discussions. The ritual basically solidifies what the family has accomplished and ritualizes it deeply in the traditions of its religious values and family heritage.

In other instances, the Family Forgiveness Ritual™ is used as a spiritual spark plug to ignite the family's compassion and spiritual traditions. In these types of situations, a roadblock has occurred, and the hope is that the grace created as a result of the ritual will generate a sufficient amount of healing to allow the family to move forward in a positive way.

When the process is utilized, it is always followed up with individual or dyadic type meetings, such as father and son or brother and sister.

From a forgiveness point of view, it's important to define what I mean by "forgiveness." There are multiple definitions, but the one I like the best is from Dr. Frederic Luskin's book *Forgive for Good*.[iv] His book is a part of the Stanford University Forgiveness Project that teaches individuals about forgiveness and demonstrates in both a before and after fashion the effects of forgiveness training. His definition of forgiveness is as follows:

> *Forgiveness is the feeling of peace that emerges as you take your hurt less personally, take responsibility for how you feel, and be-*

come a hero instead of a victim in the story you tell. Forgiveness is the experience of peacefulness in the present moment. Forgiveness does not change the past, but it changes the present. Forgiveness means that even though you are wounded, you choose to hurt and suffer less. Forgiveness means you become part of the solution. Forgiveness is the understanding that hurt is a normal part of life. Forgiveness is for you and for no one else. You can forgive and rejoin a relationship, or forgive and never speak to the person again.

In his book, Luskin talks about the benefits of forgiveness. The first benefit, and the most important one, is that forgiveness is our assertion that we are not victims of our past. It basically allows people to speak with emotional balance about the people they feel wronged by. He goes on to say: "When we forgive, we become calm enough to say confidently that what our parents taught us was dead wrong. With that calmness, we can chart the best course for our lives. Forgiveness is the beginning of a new chapter, not the end of the story."

The second benefit of learning to forgive is how we can help others—essentially by being a role model for them. The most wonderful illustration of this concept is Martin Zaidenstadt, the survivor in Timothy Ryback's book *The Last Survivor*.[v] Zaidenstadt, a Polish Jew, was shipped to Dachau in 1942. He was twenty-nine; now he's eighty-eight. After the war, he settled in the city of Dachau, an unusual thing for a survivor of the camps to do. Martin is a witness—fifty-five years after the fact. Each day he stands outside the chambers, a witness to what he knows. He knows because he was there, because he lost his wife and daughter in the camp, and because he still wakes up screaming. He knows he never left Dachau. This is what Martin had to say on forgiveness:

When people see that I have made a life in the place where I was brought to die, they understand that they, too, must learn to forgive; that if I can forgive the Germans for what they tried to do to me, they can forgive, as well.

Not only was Martin healing himself by his witness, but he was also becoming a wonderful role model for all of us in terms of the notion of forgiveness.

The third benefit of forgiveness, according to Luskin, "emerges as we give more love and care to the important people in our lives." Oscar Wilde (1854–1900) was quoted on this topic and said: "Children grow up loving their parents; as they grow older, they judge; sometimes they forgive them." In the commentary that accompanied this, the author acknowledges the benefit achieved by forgiving our parents.

Every situation has limited choices, and we work with what we've got. As adults, we realize this is exactly where our parents were when we were children. They, too, were born into an uncertain world and did the best they could. When we can forgive our parents, we are free to accept them as they are, as we might a friend. We can accept them, enjoy the relationship, and forget about collecting old debts. Making peace with them imparts to us the strength of previous generations and helps us be more at peace with ourselves.

Wilde's quote captures for me the awesome benefit of forgiveness as it applies to our parents. But the same principle can apply in all our relationships.

Essentially, what Luskin and Wilde are talking about is what I used to speak about metaphorically in my counseling sessions. When you turn the water off to your house, you turn it off at the street, and the whole house is without water. As a result, metaphorically speaking, when we hold a grievance in our heart, we lose our ability to express and receive love from those people who are so close to us.

Rabbi Zalman Schachter-Shalomi, in his book *From Age-ing to Sage-ing*,[vi] talks about the healing properties of forgiveness. He says:

> *One of the most powerful tools we have to reformat the template of our being is forgiveness . . . [W]e can reach back to repair the places of great hurt—the broken promises, the acts of betrayal, the*

ruptures and the heartache that come with the territory of intimate relationships, marriages, and divorces. All of us have unhealed emotional scar tissue that keeps our hearts closed and armored against repeated injuries.

Rabbi Zalman talks about the issue of responsibility in managing differences and forgiveness. He comments on the importance of people realizing their role, even if it's unconscious, in creating problems in families. He says:

We often fail to account for the role that we unconsciously play in creating dysfunctional relationships and situations. All too often we don't ask ourselves, "How did my hidden agenda—my expectations, unacknowledged needs, and unresolved emotional conflicts—lead to my getting hurt?" We cannot forgive the offending party as long as we have not taken responsibility for our own contribution to the misunderstanding. By portraying ourselves as victims we avoid dealing with the pain that we unconsciously inflict on ourselves. Forgiving another's deed against us requires forgiving ourselves for our complicity in the affair.

One of the key philosophical cornerstones of the ritual is self-responsibility and the notion that each one of us contributes to whatever the issues are in our families. This has often been the hardest part of the ritual for family members to accept.

Another concept of forgiveness that's important to note is what forgiveness isn't. Forgiveness does not mean condoning or accepting someone or something that hurt you. This common notion is to forgive and forget with emphasis on forgetting rather than forgiveness. It is important for people to realize that they need not continue to place themselves in situations of continual hurt or pain. When it comes to forgetting, I actually encourage clients not to forget and urge them to embrace and celebrate the hurt as a precursor to letting go.

McClendon and Kadis comment on this phenomenon in their book, *Reconciling Relationships and Preserving the Family Business*[vii]:

Moreover, forgiving does not mean that future hurtful acts done by persons who caused earlier afflictions will be excused, avoided, or ignored. Nor does it mean that permission is given for relationships to go back to the way they were before, or that past offenders are now freed from accountability for their actions. Instead, forgiving is a conscious choice to release oneself from the burden of anger and resentment, as well as from overwhelming preoccupation with hurts, which for some people can be an obsession. Forgiveness can also help others release themselves from the anger they hold toward themselves for having participated in the problem, if only as bystanders.

The idea is to remember fully, but to release yourself from the burden and pain of anger, resentment, and deep hurt. By forgiving, not only do you release yourself from this burden, but you also make it possible, by coming to a place of emotional neutrality, to allow the other to be released and open to new possibilities for the relationship. Miller comments on this concept when he states in *A Little Book of Forgiveness*: "Forgiveness allows one to share what has to change in order for the relationship to continue."

McClendon and Kadis, in their book *Reconciling Relationships and Preserving the Family Business* note, "Apologizing and forgiving are behaviors of choice—transitional acts that aid family in reestablishing necessary good will, rebuilding relationships, and refocusing on the future."

In my work, I present forgiveness to clients as a new beginning. Forgiveness allows the client system to generate the necessary goodwill to reestablish the process of building the family's emotional equity and trust. Forgiveness allows the family to create the positive emotional reservoir that is essential to survive the hard times in any family business.

The Family Forgiveness Ritual™
For the clients to understand what the Family Forgiveness Ritual™ is, I explain the different kinds of forgiveness, though the emphasis

throughout the Family Forgiveness Ritual™ is on the area of acknowledging what you've done to contribute to the problem and/or to hurt other people.

At the same time, I read a series of quotes that are designed to help people develop a positive perspective about forgiveness and to use as inspirations to assist them in identifying both the things that they have done and the things that have hurt them. The inspirations I use come from Miller's *A Little Book of Forgiveness*. He talks in the book about forgiving yourself and forgiving others—two of the most challenging things about forgiveness. His quotes on forgiving others include:

> *Begin not with the idea that you are doing a favor to someone who hurt you, but that you are being merciful to yourself. To carry an anger against anyone is to poison your own heart, administering more toxin every time you replay in your mind the injury done to you. If you decline to repeat someone's offense inwardly, your outward anger will dissipate. Then it becomes much easier to tell the one who hurt you how things must change between you.*

As I noted previously, "forgive and forget" is a popular distortion of the work of surrendering grievances. The real process is "remember fully and forgive." If it were actually possible to forget everything you forgave, you could teach very little to others seeking freedom from their resentments. When you are trying to decide whether or not someone deserves your forgiveness, you are asking the wrong question. Ask instead whether you deserve to be someone who consistently forgives.

Inspirational messages for forgiving yourself include:

- Forgiving your flaws and failures does not mean looking away from them or lying about them.

- Look at them as a string of pitiful or menacing hitchhikers whom you can't afford not to pick up on your journey to a changed life.

- Each one of them has a piece of the map you need hidden in its shabby clothing.

- You must listen attentively to all their stories and win the friendship of each one to put your map together.

- Where you are going—into a forgiven life of wholeness, passion, and commitment—you will need all the peculiar denizens of your dark side working diligently on your behalf.[viii]

In addition, I also use some quotes from *The Art of Forgiveness, Lovingkindness, and Peace*[ix] by Jack Kornfied. It is a series of meditations that allow the reader to focus on the value of forgiveness. His meditations cover forgiveness from others, forgiveness for ourselves, and forgiveness for those who have hurt or harmed us. Each one of these meditations inspires people to forgive themselves or others and makes it possible to start anew. In addition, outside the context of the Family Forgiveness Ritual™, individual discussions have usually occurred to support the positive expectations of people being successful in the forgiveness process.

The actual ritual starts with the presentation from the consultant's point of view on the nature of forgiveness and utilizes some of the previously mentioned inspirational quotes to frame the psychological perspective about forgiveness. In addition, the family's clergyperson, who has been selected by the family, shares the family's religious background, its religious philosophy of forgiveness, and how it fits into the culture of the religion and family.

The second step of the ritual is to allow people to talk about what they want to be forgiven for—what may have occurred with them that they are willing to forgive. For many families this is a very emotional part of the process. Even families that didn't anticipate they would have anything to talk about in terms of wanting to be forgiven are able to share thoughts about their contribution to the problem. Some of the most emotionally moving and positive sharing has occurred in families who thought they had nothing to share.

The next item is an absolution ritual, which has always been unique-ly different based on the religion and clergyperson involved. It's an opportunity for people to, ritualistically speaking, wash away their hurts and create a ritual of forgiveness that allows them to heal.

The next step is a Eucharistic celebration. This has been uniquely dif-ferent based on the family's religious background and clergyperson, so that each one that has been done has been different. Since the ritual has only been done with Christian families at this point, it is a format that would either be skipped or adapted for families of other religious backgrounds.

The final step of the ritual is the potluck meal. Families have tradi-tionally gathered around meals for holidays and rituals, so the Family Forgiveness Ritual™ incorporates that tradition by bringing everyone together for a potluck. In some instances that hasn't worked because of logistics, so the family has gone out to a restaurant instead. Never-theless, the culmination and celebration of the ritual is the metaphor of the banquet feast.

▮ FROM THE CASE STUDY FILES: THE DANZ FAMILY

The first attempt at this ritual occurred in November 1998 with the Danz family—a family that had been plagued by family business troubles for many years and had made several previous attempts to resolve their differences but had not been successful.

The presenting problem was the fact that the father and his oldest son, Brian, who worked in the business, could not agree on how the business should be run. They were constantly arguing, and after many years of this, the daughter, Martha, who worked with them in the business, finally decided she was unwilling to continue unless her father and brother worked out their differences.

One of the unique characteristics of this family had to do with the father's name, which was Wimp. I refused to call him that until I realized its significance. Wimp's father, as it turned out, was a butcher, and when he would go to work each morning, he would ask what his son would like for dinner, and his son would reply, "Hamburger." His dad would reply, "That's my Wimp," referring to Wimpy in the Popeye cartoon.

As it turned out, Wimp's father died when he was ten years old, and that was his most enduring memory of his father. When I understood this and realized the name's significance, I was also able to understand the issues between Wimp and Brian and redefined the problem as an issue of loss. Wimp had lost his father to a heart attack when he was a young boy; Brian had lost his father to business tensions. As I began to talk about that issue with the family members who were participating in the engagement, which included Wimp, the mother, Brian and his wife, and Martha, each of them identified loss issues in their family. As a result of sharing that, we were able to create some positive innovations and move forward in the short space of three or four meetings.

However, in addition to that, there was a bigger issue having to do with the vilification of Brian by the other two children in the family. When I suggested to the family that was the problem and recommended the Family Forgiveness Ritual™ and the use of their pastor, they were eager to proceed. I made my presentation on the psychological aspects of forgiveness, and the pastor made his observations from a religious perspective. The Danz family was a conservative, traditional Catholic family, and the priest was a Benedictine monk. His remarks were able to draw on the Church's longstanding tradition of forgiveness, and he shared a very positive perspective about it with the Danz family.

When it came time for people to talk about what they wanted to be forgiven for, there was a very, very long silence. I had thoughts running through my mind about whether this was the right thing to do, until the silence was broken by the second son, Ken, who had flown in from Memphis to participate in the ritual. He said to his father, "I want to ask your forgiveness for taking so long to tell you that I was gay." He had previously shared with his family that he was gay but was now asking for forgiveness for taking so long and not trusting his parents.

After another very long silence, Wimp responded, "I want to ask your forgiveness for how I handled hearing that you were gay." At that point, the mother began to cry, and each family member in turn went around sharing what he or she had contributed to the problem.

The priest then conducted an absolution ritual and the home Eucharist. It was followed by a potluck meal that the family had prepared.

The ritual started at nine that morning, and at seven that evening when the family was cleaning up, many of them were sitting in the living room reminiscing about family stories. Brian, who at the beginning of the ritual was isolated in a corner, was now the heart of the family sharing.

That Christmas, Ken brought his partner home for the first time, and the Danz's had the best Christmas they had ever had.

In February 2004, I talked with the mother, who indicated that the family was getting together to celebrate their fiftieth wedding anniversary. In that conversation, she mentioned the business was doing very well and the family had never been better. As a matter of fact, she said the whole family was getting ready to leave for a cruise to celebrate their anniversary.

In other families, the absolution ritual has been different. One of the more dramatic instances of this was done with a Presbyterian minister and a family where there had been deep hurts because of business differences.

The absolution ritual included the distribution and collection of family IOUs and an explanation by the minister that the original

"Our Father" was worded in terms of debts—"forgive us our debts as we forgive those who have debted against us." He explained that in the Old Testament, when you offended someone, not only were you emotionally indebted to them, but you were also financially indebted. The use of the IOUs was a wonderful symbolism that allowed the family to get beyond the hurts and create healing and move forward.

In another family, the absolution ritual included olive oil that was blessed by the priest who was conducting the ceremony. Family members dipped their thumbs in the olive oil and blessed one another with the sign of the cross saying, "God's forgiveness, our forgiveness, love."

So you can see, the ritual changes based on the family, but the result is a healing process that allows the family to start anew in a positive way and go forward. Although I recommend Family Forgiveness Rituals™ regularly, there are some families who have been reluctant to do them. Several instances have occurred where other professionals, even psychological professionals, have advised a family that they're not ready to participate in such a ritual. My belief is that participating in the ritual opens the door to positive healing within the family that changes their perspective and that it's not necessary to wait until people are completely ready. My belief is that the ritual itself has an inspirational message that allows people to go beyond their hurts to move forward in a positive way. I believe Frederic Luskin's work at Stanford supports the conclusion that people can be taught to forgive, and the results are measurable thereafter.

There are some families where participating in a Family Forgiveness Ritual™ has not been successful. In one such instance, the family was so steeped in its hurt and wounds that they were unwilling to give up their despair and hurt to move forward in a positive way. Unfortunately, as this chapter is being written, they are embroiled in litigation where their mutual hurts are being fought over in a courtroom.

Family Forgiveness Rituals™ are an opportunity for family members who have been hurt or broken by business and financial differences to create healing in their families and to short circuit the distance, anguish, and hurt that often occurs. The success of the ritual is a function of the family's ability to draw on their deep well of emotional and family traditions, as well as their religious traditions. In doing so, they are able to utilize the internal wisdom of their family and move forward in a positive and caring way to create a new beginning.

Managing Conflict in a Family-Owned Business

Death, money, and sex. In our culture, these are the three most difficult things for families to talk about. They are forbidden topics no matter who you are, how old you are, what you do, or how much you earn. Virtually everyone avoids talking about death, money, and sex in their families. Do you?

Unfortunately, when a family-owned business is having a conflict, it is likely that two of these topics must be talked about—death and money. That's because conflict in a successful family business commonly occurs when it's time for succession planning—when the family must decide who will continue the business and how. Many families make the mistake of just assuming who will take over the company and that succession will happen when the time is right. That's where the problems begin.

Estate planners tell us succession is a highly unpleasant subject for families. It requires them to think about death in the family, life without a loved one, taking or transferring assets, and changing responsibilities. For a family business, the discussion seems especially filled with potential landmines.

Family businesses avoid succession planning
Succession planning is not only an issue for the owner-entrepreneur, but it's also an issue for the entire family. Many families unconsciously conspire to avoid talking about ownership and management succession planning. The topic is taboo.

My clients will say, "It's too early; we have years to think about this." Or, "I don't have time right now." Succession planning is crucial in family business because it helps you avoid the emotional tripwires and makes the rational path more visible. However, that path must include more than just plans for ownership and the estate.

It is futile to produce a succession plan by focusing on the ownership (and estate) plan. A smart succession plan must also consider the owner-entrepreneur's overall intention. It must reflect a core purpose that includes legacy and family intentions, as well as the business purpose.

Legacy is more than an entrepreneur's wish for how he or she wants to be remembered. A sense of legacy drives the entrepreneur to develop a succession plan. Concern for a legacy creates the motivation.

Start by discussing legacy

I use Hubler's Legacy Model™ to help set the base and develop the discussion for successful succession plans. There are two aspects to legacy: your gift to the future and how you want to be remembered. The first aspect, discussed by Laura Nash and Howard Stevenson in the *Harvard Business Review* article "Success that Lasts,"[x] defines your gift to the future as a means by which you help others find future success.

The second aspect, how you want to be remembered, is where my definition comes in. It focuses more personally on how an individual wants to be remembered and is

Source: Laura Nash & Howard Stevenson, 2004

highly emotional because virtually everyone in their sixties and seventies wonders at some point whether their lives have meant something. They may avoid talking or thinking about it, but it's there.

A technical planner can ask:

- How do you want to be remembered?

- What is your gift to the future?

- How can I help you achieve those goals?

Ask legacy questions like these so that owner-entrepreneurs will engage in succession planning. This helps avoid a lot of unnecessary conflict that could surface later.

Some Specks of Dust™ that can become family-business issues:

- Family values regarding wealth

- Financial distributions to shareholders

- Disputes about roles, responsibilities, and decision-making

- Governance

- Business plan

- Business and financial differences

- Roles of parents and grandparents

- Roles of in-laws (daughters- and sons-in-law, in particular)

- Training — competency

- Control

- Boundaries

- Prenuptials

- Commitment to the company and work

- Win-lose decision-making

- Hurt feelings, listening, and understanding

- Unmet wants and expectations

- Indirect communication (gossiping behind someone's back)

- Lack of expression of appreciation, recognition, and love

- Loss and change

- Spending

- Sibling rivalry

- Lack of structure and formality

The price of peacekeeping

One of the driving forces for entrepreneurs and their families is family unity, but conflict can occur because family members try to avoid it. An issue might seem trivial at first, but small problems ignored become very large problems.

As I mentioned in Chapter 2, an issue or irritation can trigger differences in the family-owned business. When families gather and there are minor business or financial differences, family members often think, "We're all going to the lake for the Fourth of July; I don't want to create a family problem by bringing up our issues because it will ruin everything." Nothing is said, and that speck of dust—that issue—is not discussed. Time passes; it's Labor Day, then it's Thanksgiving, then it's Hanukkah or Christmas. Every time the family gets together, the small problems are ignored, and instead of going away, they fester, eventually growing into larger, more serious issues.

Family members inadvertently create the very problem they're trying to avoid by not discussing business and financial differences. To avoid conflict, most families try to compromise or give up things they care about to keep the peace. I understand how this can happen; as a young boy, I was taught to do the same. But experience has taught me that compromising and giving things up doesn't really work.

Every family and family-owned business has issues. It's important to remember that these little issues are normal and need to be aired. Minor issues become problems only when they are avoided and not discussed.

How to prevent and manage problems in family-owned businesses

The best way to prevent conflict is to keep issues from becoming problems in the first place. To do this, the family should create a Common Family Vision™ that unites everyone at a superordinate level. How might that be done?

Typically, one would urge compromise as the way to create unity in a family. Yet when individuals are asked to compromise, they generally feel like they are conceding or giving in. Instead, the family should be encouraged to understand that this is a negotiation that involves cooperation. Everyone is working together for the common good of the family and the business—high stakes, indeed.

Individuals recognize that it is unrealistic for each person to get everything he or she wants. Instead, each family member is contributing to reflect what's best for the family vision. Each individual gives out of love, generosity, a sense of abundance, and trust. Each understands that other members of the family will contribute in the same way when their turn comes. And the others' turns always come.

The Common Family Vision™, discussed in detail in Chapter 2, is an excellent tool to help in these situations. These high-level principles are discussed and developed into a brief paragraph that truly reflects what the family believes about themselves and their values. Some families think of them as mission statements.

Also discussed earlier, kything can be used to manage conflict. I encourage family members to think about one another daily through brief kything. Kythes are the vision statements of family members that are written in the third person and reflect what that person wants, needs, or values.

Earlier I discussed how important it is to raise issues, prepare succession plans, and create a Common Family Vision™. This form and structure helps unite family members in a superordinate goal. Now I will introduce other specific methods to bring structure to family-business issues and to prevent conflict.

Who's the B.O.S.S.?

Remember the B.O.S.S. concept? It's a way to remember what the family wants to generate for the . . .

Business
Others (and what you want for them regarding what they want)
Self (what you want for yourself)
Stakeholders (including others who share in the business)

The least intuitive of these is recognizing that in order to prevent issues from becoming problems, you must identify what the Others want. Every family member must understand that they have a commitment to one another's success. This is what defines a team with people who consciously help one another succeed. In this way, kything and the "O" in B.O.S.S. mean the same thing.

Being aware of others unleashes energy because there is psychological engagement within the family. It is strikingly portrayed by author Mihaly Csikszentmihalyi. I summarize his concept with a few quotes taken from his book *Finding Flow*:[xi]

- *An optimal family system is complex in that it encourages the unique individual development of its members while uniting them in a web of effective ties.*

- *A group of people is kept together by two kinds of energy —material energy provided by food, warmth, physical care, and money, and the psychic energy of people investing attention in each other's goals.*

- *When people pay attention to each other or to the same activity together, the chances of finding flow, binding the family, increase.*

- *Only when there is harmony between the goals of the participants, when everyone is investing psychic energy into a joint goal, does being together become enjoyable.*

Csikszentmihalyi emphasizes the importance of putting psychic energy into families. He is talking about regular families, not those involved in business or wealth. I would suggest that the need for this engagement is even greater for business families where strained relationships can produce even greater consequences. The point is that good things happen when people are committed to one another's success.

Develop Collaborative Team Skills

An excellent way to prevent conflict is to strengthen family communications using Sherod Miller's Collaborative Team Skills.[xii] As I mentioned earlier, the program helps people learn how to express feelings and wants. When these deep needs go unexpressed, communication breaks down. I consider listening skills to be the most important way to promote understanding within the family.

Proper listening requires knowing how to respond to different communication styles, map an issue, and actively problem solve. Conflict often arises because people don't listen carefully or they respond poorly. A few simple techniques can sidestep a lot of misunderstanding.

Hold regular family meetings

In his book *Family Business* (3rd ed.), Ernesto Poza[xiii] promotes family meetings. He states that when family businesses have regular family meetings, they become more successful. This promise of greater success is reason enough to meet regularly as a family.

As I've noted previously, successful family-owned businesses typically hold three types of meetings:

1. Shareholder and owner meetings that include only those members

2. Meetings designed for employees and family member stakeholders

3. Family meetings that bring together the entire family, including spouses and those not active in the business

Each type of meeting has its own dynamic, purpose, and value. Family meetings, in particular, help manage the boundary between family and business. This is where so many potential conflicts can be discussed and resolved. Family meetings build the emotional equity of the family (the psychic energy of *Finding Flow*) while simultaneously building the equity of the business.

Here are a few of the many ways to build emotional equity in the family:

- Establish and celebrate family rituals and traditions

- Regularly spend informal time with one another outside of the business

- Involve adult children and grandchildren in family-oriented services and philanthropic projects

Prepare a Family Participation Plan™

Issues raised and resolved in family meetings can be restated as part of a Family Participation Plan™. Too many family-owned businesses regularly play the game of business without having or regularly reviewing their own sets of ground rules. Or they assume the rules are unchanged and fail to keep them current.

I use this outline with my clients to guide them to their own Family Participation Plans™:

- Eligibility

- Entry

- Summer employment

- Intern programs

- Non-family executives

- Full-time employees

- Career planning

- Application process

- Coaching

- Poor performance and termination

- Conduct and protocol

- Compensation

Discomfort around touchy issues is natural in every family and family business. Holding regular family meetings and producing a Family Participation Plan™ can prevent many of these issues from becoming problems. My mantra for clients can't be repeated too often: "It's always easier to prevent a problem than to try to fix one." Conflicts become painful only if ignored.

The Silent Treatment

Avoiding the discussion of family disagreements simply magnifies problems. Families that don't discuss their business differences to preserve family harmony are making a painful mistake.

Communicating and managing differences are fundamental to a civil society, an effective workplace, and a happy family. But when your business associates are also your family members, it can get complicated. As I've mentioned before, families may avoid communicating about differences to sidestep major arguments.

If you're part of a family business—even as a non-family employee— you may have seen this dynamic. A son who is at odds with his father about how to run the business, but he doesn't bring it up because it will spoil an upcoming family gathering. Or brothers who don't share their disagreement over their roles in the company because it will upset their family at Thanksgiving or Christmas. So when there's serious disagreement, individuals in a family may stuff it and try to wait it out.

This is seldom a wise approach. When we avoid talking about our differences, we magnify the problem we're trying to avoid—it's Hubler's Speck of Dust Theory™ again, a recurring theme when talking about conflict.

The enforced silence of not sharing disagreements can escalate into the silent treatment. Family members become so annoyed that they refuse to speak to one another. The reasoning is that by not speaking to someone you're punishing them. Of course, that reasoning travels both ways. The silent treatment is not only unproductive, but it also adds to frustration and hurt feelings.

FROM THE CASE STUDY FILES: THE HARRIS FAMILY

When I met the Harris family, Walter and his son Ted had not spoken to each other in four years. That's right—four years. Yet they labored side by side five days a week. They ran all of their communication through Pat, Walter's youngest son and Ted's brother, who also worked in the company.

When Pat finally said, "If you two can't get your acts together, I'm out of here," his demand became the impetus for hiring me. We got to work.

I learned that the breakdown began those long years ago when Walter voiced his disapproval of Ted's wife, Jean. He said disrespectful things. Ted shut down, and the silent treatment began. This was the typical way they "resolved" differences in their family; they stopped talking to each other.

I met with Walter and Ted five or six times over the summer. We made progress. They were able to discuss their hurts, understand what they expected of one another, and discover what they needed from one another to thrive as business partners, as well as father and son.

By the fall, they were working well together. The company was operating smoothly, and they were again enjoying social time after work. However, during my conversations with Walter, Ted, and then others, larger issues emerged. The adult children blamed their brother Ted for issues at the company. They had given him the silent treatment at family gatherings and holidays. Ted and Jean felt isolated. It was evident that the entire family had to get involved to work this through.

In reality, it's impossible to live in a family with people you love and not step on one another's toes. That was when I suggested they try the Family Forgiveness Ritual™. Tears mingled with smiles, and losses became gains. Each had shared what mattered, spoken their truth, and asked for forgiveness. Each heard and responded to the others. The silence had ended. It was their new beginning.

Emotional Equity

Like any business, a family business strives to build the equity of the company. However, as a business family, shareholders have a second concern: to build the emotional equity of the family. Whether the business of the family is large or small, has multiple branches or is simply a little start-up, it requires a commitment to strengthen family relationships and build family trust.

One way that works well to build relationships and trust is when the family divides its family meeting time between conducting business and having fun. Informal as well as organized fun activities build family harmony. Some families hold a family meeting at a special place such as Disney World. These family trips may not occur every year, but they provide such positive experiences that they are a topic of happy conversation for years.

Another way to build the emotional equity of the shareholders is to combine family time with business activity by holding an annual family retreat. I know of a family that brings everyone together at the family cabin each year. While the adults are in their meeting, the grandmother hires several summer camp counselors to do arts and crafts with the grandchildren, who love the opportunity to get together with their cousins. Time is set aside where the grandparents share their history with their grandchildren. At one such meeting, the grandparents began by showing photographs of themselves when they were younger and told stories about those years ago—how they met, dated, married, and managed. The grandchildren sat spellbound as they listened and asked questions. The entire experience with the grandparents was videotaped and made into a DVD for each of the families.

These are a few examples of how families build emotional equity. I've also seen families involve adult children and grandchildren in service projects. In this way, grandparents not only demonstrate family values of gratitude, but they also bring the family together to create priceless memories. Given the complexities of all of our lives, it is important for the younger shareholders to take an active role in creating family activities and not rely solely on the initiative of their parents.

Business families have the extra challenge to build their family's emotional equity and not neglect it in the day-to-day demands of running their business. For business families it is not easy to separate work life from home life because the family is the business. As a result, the family needs to consciously discuss and share family values, family heritage, and involve the entire family in service and philanthropic work.

As shareholders discuss their roles in creating the future of their business family, the conversation will inevitably move to stewardship and legacy. While it is important for the younger shareholders to draw from their parents' energy for connecting the siblings and cousins, an equal amount of energy to build the emotional equity of the family needs to come from the younger generation of shareholders. The true legacy of any business family is not merely a stronger business, but a stronger family, as well.

Building the shareholder legacy of family harmony is a gift to the future, and not only for the family—research indicates it is a significant gift, one that shows up in the profits of the business. At your next family meeting, include a discussion of the ways to strengthen your family's emotional equity. I know you will not regret it.

Alcoholism's "Stinkin' Thinkin'"

I recall a particularly difficult client report I once had to write. It was about an upcoming family planning meeting, and the dynamics of the situation were highly complex because there was chemical abuse in the family. It was the elephant in the room that the family would not address, yet it influenced—in fact, drove—the tone of the family planning session itself.

When alcohol or other chemical addiction is a part of the dynamic in a family, virtually any attempt to resolve family and business issues is infinitely more difficult. From my experience, alcohol is one of the most difficult issues to solve in the context of family business succession planning. Unfortunately, addiction is such a powerful influence that many, if not most, families (and individuals) would rather deny it exists than deal with the problem.

Addiction can make people overly defensive, confrontational, and even bullying and irrational. As a young post-graduate student, I participated in a training program on the diagnosis, treatment, and understanding of chemical dependency. Harry Swift, one of the early staff members of the now-famous Hazelden Betty Ford Addiction Treatment Center in Minnesota, was giving a lecture, and he identified the irrational thinking that occurs in a family where addiction is a problem as "Stinkin' Thinkin'"—a term that has stayed with me ever since. It's the crazy, distorted, delusional mindset an addict can have. I have dealt with this often in my practice. Here is an example that demonstrates how dysfunctional it can be.

I had arrived to begin the second day of the Riley clan's two-day family business planning meeting at the Riley family cabin located on a picturesque lake in upstate New York. On the first day, we focused on identifying the issues and challenges facing the Riley family and the business they owned. On the second day, the plan was to create a Riley Common Family Vision™ designed to unite them. I had also planned on introducing them to the Collaborative Team Skills process as a way to strengthen the family's communication skills and help them better manage their differences.

I arrived first, before the adult children. As I walked into the cabin, the patriarch, Vincent, who was standing in the kitchen, summoning me to follow him. We entered a bedroom aglow with sunshine streaming through glass patio doors that overlooked the lake. And then Vincent turned and proceeded to chew me out.

"I hired you to fix Alex and Bob (his sons)," he said. "Not to focus on me." This was how he began what became a half-hour rant. The experience reminded me of when I was a little boy and my father (who was an alcoholic) took me "to the woodshed" in my parents' bedroom.

As a result of my participation in Adult Children of Alcoholics, Al-Anon, and my professional training, I saw Vincent's behavior for what it was—a cry for help. I understood why it surfaced—because some of this addiction-driven behavior had come up during discussions on the first day.

A LITTLE BACKGROUND . . .

Vincent and his wife, Marg, were semi-retired and lived on their boat in Florida during the winters. Their sons, Alex and Bob, were tapped to run the company. Vincent had expressed concerns about their leadership capabilities and said he had lost confidence in them. I recognized those concerns as typical in a family business when there is no formal agreement between first- and second-generation executives—in this case between Vincent and his adult children. The lack of formality often hinders financial performance for the company and strains parent-child relationships.

Also during that first day, the two sons had talked about Vincent and Marg's heavy use of alcohol. This was what got Vincent steaming. When they were on their boat in Florida, Vincent and Marg would have a bottle or two of wine with dinner. Then they would call their sons in New York to talk to the grandchildren. Alex and Bob and their wives would not let Vincent and Marg talk to their children when they were slurring their words and under the influence.

At that point, I suggested that since the family shared a concern about the parents' alcohol use, the simple solution was for Vincent and Marg to have an assessment to determine if there was a problem and then take it from there. Vincent's half-hour "discussion" with me the second morning of the retreat was his rationalization for why he and Marg were backing away from the commitment they had made the previous day to have the assessment done.

The time he spent telling me why I should focus on the sons and not on him put everything behind schedule for the second day. The meeting ended on a positive note, but the question about whether Vincent and Marg would have an alcohol assessment was left unanswered.

In telephone calls with Alex and Bob later, I learned that the parents did not address it, nor did the rest of the family. If they did not address their concerns about alcohol abuse, it would certainly have a damaging effect on their lives.

Alcohol misuse blurs boundaries, and it undermines the family and its effectiveness when it comes to running a business. It reduces the ability to problem solve and magnifies differences while diminishing the ability to communicate and manage them. What's more, for the Riley family, alcohol misuse seriously diminished their capacity for emotional intimacy.

Our two-day session exposed the drinking problem, and all the adult family members agreed that a simple assessment would provide a starting point for resolving it. But the very nature of alcoholism's "stinkin' thinkin'" kept the family from doing what was rational and put the addiction ahead of the family, the business, and the future.

The lesson here is that if you suspect someone in your family is abusing a substance, the first step is to encourage—aggressively encourage—that person to have a professional evaluation. That's when healing can begin.

FROM THE CASE STUDY FILES: THE OLSON FAMILY

So how does the healing process begin? Here we'll explore how one courageous family dealt with chemical abuse and got the family and the business back on track.

Like the Riley family, the Olson family business also was affected by the abuse of alcohol—and drugs.

Some history: Paul Olson started the family business in his basement with his wife, Sally, as the bookkeeper and right-hand person. When their oldest daughter, Patti, graduated from college, she joined the business. Eventually Patti married, and her husband, Gary, an attorney, was invited to join the business. Paul and Sally's son Erik also joined the business after receiving his graduate degree in a field unrelated to the family business. Lars, the youngest son, struggled to find himself. He had not completed college and worked on the periphery, running errands for the business.

Gary received a generous salary from the business but was not following through on his responsibilities in the sales department. Gary had declined to hear or respond to any feedback. Then, pornography was discovered on Gary's laptop and, at the urging of Paul and Sally, Gary and Patti went to see a marriage counselor.

I was asked to work with the family because of Gary's performance. As I was conducting the Olson family business planning meeting, we were able to identify and discuss the key issues facing the business. In my experience, the issues were typical and resolvable, and they included a lack of formalized performance appraisals, compensation systems, and career/training programs for the next generation entering the business.

Informally during that session, the parents also expressed a loving concern about the use of alcohol and marijuana by their adult children.

We went to a restaurant for the lunch break. After the waitress took our food and beverage orders, Patti ordered a glass of wine. I told Patti that it was not a good idea to have any alcohol while we were having the family planning meeting and discussing such sensitive issues. When I suggested she have a soft drink instead, she blew up at me, left the table in a fury, and refused to rejoin the family lunch. Later, Patti returned to join us after some coaching from her parents.

We started the afternoon session by reviewing the issues and recommendations from earlier in the day. It also came up that in addition to Patti's alcohol misuse, her brothers, Erik and Lars, were smoking marijuana every day. At that point Patti jumped up, left the room, and did not return.

Frustrated, the parents, Paul and Sally, halted the session and postponed going forward with the family meeting. Paul, Sally, and I then decided that the next step was to hold a family seminar on alcohol and drug abuse. It would be conducted by a trained alcohol and drug abuse counselor, with the entire family attending.

Following the chemical abuse seminar, Erik made a personal commitment to stop his drug use. Patti and her husband, Gary, refused to acknowledge that there was a problem. Soon afterward, Patti cut off contact with her parents and would not give them access to their grandchildren. Gary resigned from the business, saying he and Patti were putting their home up for sale and moving to another state.

As one would imagine, Paul and Sally were devastated by this. Yet, courageously, they began to participate in Al-Anon, a twelve-step program to learn more about addiction. Also by my recommendation, they stopped using alcohol themselves to be role models for their children and grandchildren.

Several months after Gary and Patti had moved to a new city, Patti contacted her parents to say she wanted to move home. Gary had filed for divorce. Amid those unfortunate circumstances, Paul and Sally were delighted that she would move back and bring the grandchildren. They supported her so she could set up a new residence close to them. Patti continued to see her counselor and eventually began participating in Alcoholics Anonymous. As I write this, she has been sober for ten years.

POSITIVE OUTCOMES

The Olson family business continues to grow and thrive. I helped them overcome their business issues, as well as recognize and respond to their personal ones. The adult children continue to grow and mature in their roles at the company. Erik is the heir-apparent and is being groomed to take over as president when Paul retires. Lars eventually went back to college to get a degree and now works successfully outside of the family business.

This life-changing shift was made possible because we helped guide each family member to summon the courage to address, take action, and resolve the issues facing them. "Stinkin' Thinkin'" makes individuals irrational and abrasive, and their family is left walking on eggshells. They feel the unease but are in denial about it. They are afraid to lose one another's love or respect. They don't want to rock the boat. They imagine only bad consequences will result from addressing the problem, not realizing that if left unchecked, chemical abuse will always lead to bad outcomes.

Wherever there is chemical abuse, there is a huge loss in family intimacy, communication, management effectiveness, and the ability to achieve problem resolution. This loss is magnified because the business is the family, and effective relationships are the platform on which the continued success of both rests.

Betrayal: The Emotional Malady of Family Businesses

There may be no more debilitating force than betrayal when it occurs in a family business. Poet William Blake (1757–1827) wrote, "It is easier to forgive an enemy than to forgive a friend." That's because every betrayal begins with trust. It is "a violence against confidence," an inside job. In my experience, betrayal ranks as a top destroyer of otherwise-successful business families.

By its technical definition, betrayal breaks or violates a presumed contract, trust, or expectation to produce moral and psychological conflict in a relationship between individuals, organizations, or both. But this cool, reasoned description of betrayal misses its intensity. Of all possible tragedies in life (except the death of a loved one), betrayal can wound more painfully than things physical; pierce more deeply than other things emotional; and devastate love, trust, and loyalty beyond what would seem endurable. When betrayal occurs among family members engaged in a family business, the loss can be unimaginable. I have witnessed its crushing effects in my work with business families.

▇ FROM THE CASE STUDY FILES: THE BROWN FAMILY

Jack Brown was mentoring his thirty-three-year-old daughter, Meredith, in the family business. Meredith had been working in the business for five years and had gained her father's trust and confidence.

A decade earlier, Jack had divorced his wife, Leslie (Meredith's mother), and remarried. Leslie had become unhappy with the divorce settlement and took Jack back to court.

During the settlement dispute, Meredith told her mother some private, sensitive financial information about Jack's business. Jack was shocked and distraught by his daughter's betrayal. He fired Meredith. Their father-daughter relationship was shattered and they no longer speak to each other.

This is one example among many situations that I have heard about or been part of in which differences between family members—strategic disagreements, leadership disputes, vendor arrangements, financial provisions, future business directions, buy-sell decisions, etc.—have been stunned by betrayal that caused irreparable harm and ruined relationships. On the surface these differences may sound like typical business negotiations, but when family is involved and expectations are unspoken, hurt feelings cut more deeply. Misunderstandings are seen as betrayal. Emotional distress damages relationships and generates destructive consequences to both the family and the business.

Betrayal can be so damaging in a family business that trust and confidence are never restored. A betrayal may be forgiven but not forgotten and can continue to erode the relationship. There is no way to undo the desolation of betrayal, no calm compromise, no meeting of the minds. As playwright Arthur Miller (1915–2005) put it, "Betrayal is the only truth that sticks."

Reconciliation seems impossible because it's not "just business"—it's personal. That's why business families must learn to anticipate the unthinkable by having ways to preempt these situations and to learn how to heal hurts once they occur.

Prevent. And if you don't prevent, heal.

Forgiving begins to soothe betrayal
Betrayal is a powerful emotion best soothed by a combination of other emotions that can help a family overcome the mistrust, blame, and incredible pain that can tear apart business families. These emotional centers are acceptance, compassion, forgiveness, and gratitude.

- **Acceptance** starts when we understand that there are situations in our lives that we can't control. Accepting that in some instances we are powerless is a major healing factor in relationships. We recognize that we can control only our own response to what happens. In the Brown family, Jack fired his daughter and has yet to accept his role in their shattered relationship.

- **Compassion** helps us understand that a person is more than the sum of his or her faults. Each of us has positive and negative aspects to our personalities. Betrayers have both positive and negative qualities, too. By focusing on both sides, we can begin to forgive. This also helps relieve our own suffering and pain.

- **Forgiveness** can seed a new beginning in our relationship with a betrayer. Forgiveness allows us to understand that "to be wrong is nothing, unless you remember it," as was so wisely stated by Confucius. Forgiveness helps clean the slate for you and others. Because family members love one another, forgiveness is essential so that relationships can be renewed after a betrayal.

- **Gratitude** is the recognition that our lives are blessed and that we need to express appreciation for the abundance we receive. There is always a choice: to focus on the negative in our lives or to focus on the blessings and good things that happen to us. As Mahatma Gandhi (1869–1948) said, "Nobody can hurt me without my permission." This is the approach each participant in the Family Forgiveness Ritual™ takes by choosing to focus on his or her blessings.

Putting these four emotions into action helps both the betrayed and the betrayer begin the healing process and refresh their relationship. By making this choice and taking responsibility for our responses, we create an inner peace and do not allow hurts and betrayals in our lives to overcome us.

Of course, the preferred approach is to prevent or reduce the capacity for betrayal in the first place. That is made more possible by structuring the family business in such a way as to avoid it.

Prevention is always better than intervention

As previously discussed, family-owned businesses often lack structure because, too often, family members confuse formality with mistrust. "We don't need rules," they say, "because we love one another." Yet that is precisely why a business family needs clear agreements.

Too much informality gets people in trouble. Meredith, the daughter who was fired, should not have had access to the company's financial information so early in her career. But because she was family, she saw information that would not have been available to non-family employees working their way up in the business. Restricting access would have prevented the problem from occurring.

The Brown family put individual disagreements ahead of business effectiveness. An impartial board of directors with outside advisors could help prevent these dysfunctions. A more formal contract describing each family member's responsibilities and duties would set parameters and define roles. Additional education, skill development, and leadership mentoring would help nurture the capabilities of individual family members. Unless this is done consciously and formally, it is left to chance, and the business and the family will suffer.

Betrayal is most devastating when it occurs with someone you love. It is doubly disheartening when the betrayer is both a family member and a co-worker.

There is no complete antidote for betrayal. I'll repeat my mantra again, "It is easier to prevent a problem than to try to fix one," and business families can inoculate themselves with structure, clearly defined roles, checks and balances, and love that chooses to forgive the impact of betrayal.

From the start, Mary Howard worked side-by-side with her husband, Tom, on their manufacturing business. He worked outside and handled all of the production; Mary managed work inside and kept the books. Their business thrived, and all four of their adult children worked in the business.

When Tom died unexpectedly at a young age, Mary inherited control of the entire company with a new role as chairman of the board, and her four children took on greater responsibilities. Her oldest, Tim, took charge of production. Her daughter, Kitty, tackled accounting and the books. The middle son, Dennis, became company president. And Joe, the youngest, worked with his oldest brother to help manage the production department. Although Mary was the board chair, she also was their mother, and she got caught between the business and her adult children over the issue of compensation.

Dennis was particularly upset. He was the president and the company's public face, but he made less money than Tim, who managed production. Mary had decided to pay Tim the most since he was the oldest child. She also reasoned that he should get the most because he had more children and needed extra money to raise them.

Dennis felt betrayed by Mary's decision and felt he was being treated unprofessionally. The situation also made Dennis and Tim upset with each other. They were at a stalemate because family sensitivities were interfering with business formalities.

I recommended to the Howards that they needed a compensation plan that included a Family Participation Plan™. This approach would establish the ground rules the family needed to run their family business.

In this case, I encouraged Mary and the family to adopt a compensation plan based on the four Ps of compensation: position, performance, percentile, and premium. The four Ps model recognizes the position's level of criticality, performance by the family member, what the position should be paid, and whether the family member receives a premium due to family status.

We had Mary work with an accountant to establish the pay range for the positions her adult children held. Then we suggested she determine what she would pay each position in that range. Next, we asked Mary to establish performance criteria for each of the positions so that each adult child knew what it took to do the job well and what bonus they would receive for that achievement. Last, we advised Mary to determine whether the adult children would receive a pay premium simply because they were family members.

Mary followed our advice and formalized the compensation program. What started as a mother caught in the middle, torn between practical business needs and emotional family dynamics, culminated in her transformation into a positive balance for her family and the business.

Mary implemented the necessary structure and formality for the business while preserving her family's relationships. I'm happy to report that Dennis reconciled with his mother, and Dennis and Tim recognized the value of each other as business partners and brothers. Both the business and family are thriving.

5

CHANGING OF THE GUARD (SUCCESSION PLANNING)

The Ten Most Prevalent Obstacles of Family Business Succession Planning

In a presentation at the University of St. Thomas Center for Family Enterprise Family Business Forum, John Davis, a family business consultant, researcher, and educator, commented that everything consultants such as himself teach, their clients already know. In order to be successful, they need to confront or deal with the obstacles. Of course, the first question that popped into my mind was: What are those issues or obstacles? As I looked back over my practice, I began to identify some of the most common obstacles.

The following ten obstacles are derived from my observations of client situations that became stumbling blocks and obstructed their ability to move from their current state to successfully navigate the succession planning process:

#10: Poor expression of feelings and wants
The failure to express feelings and wants exists in most family-owned business situations. This omission is one of the major predictors of poor and ineffective communication. To communicate effectively, people need to be vulnerable, and that is the issue. In many family businesses, the family does not have the capability, experience, or confidence to be able to express their feelings and wants around the

other daunting obstacles that follow. In some instances, their experience has been so frustrating and unproductive that they give up and are no longer willing to take the risk of vulnerability. As a result, the stumbling block occurs.

Also, in our culture and in many families, we are taught not to express our feelings and wants. I grew up being taught not to express my wants. I remember, as a small boy, when we would visit relatives I would tell them I wanted a piece of candy from the dish on the coffee table. I was immediately told that it was more polite to wait until it was offered. I waited and waited and waited, but no one offered it to me.

That is exactly what happens in family-owned businesses where family members have expectations of one another about what they want in an emotional sense. They are reluctant to express it, and no one offers it, so they think they're not worthy.

The solution I use with my clients is to engage them in a communication training process that allows them to become more familiar with and confident about being able to express their feelings and wants. The Collaborative Team Skills workbook[i] is an excellent resource for clients. They are able to learn in a relatively short period of time the necessary skills to transcend this obstacle.

#9: Differences are seen as a liability rather than an asset
Differences are really the key to an exciting and active life, but often in family-owned businesses, differences are interpreted as "you don't love me" and "you don't care." In other instances, differences are personalized with the same kind of result.

I use the Myers-Briggs Type Inventory[ii] as a resource tool to help people understand and objectify the notion of differences. I find that it helps me teach people in a positive way about their differences and how they can use the synergy among them to create a third or fourth way of doing things that they otherwise would not have considered.

#8: Indirect communication

One of the most insidious problems in family-owned businesses is the use of indirect communication. When differences occur, as they often do in succession planning, it is almost always a problem if people do not talk with one another directly. Family members involved in the business often talk indirectly with other family members who are not involved. This creates a triangle that destroys the quality of family relationships. Again, I use the Collaborative Team Skills workbook, especially the chapter on styles of communication, as a resource to educate clients about the pitfalls of indirect communication and to assist them in communicating directly for a win-win result.

#7: Entitlement

Often entitlement is seen as a younger-generation issue. Certainly that is true when younger-generation family members use their name as a wedge or variance to achieve advantage over other people in the organization. When this occurs, it has a negative effect on morale. In a recent client situation, a thirty-year-old second-generation member of a family-owned business was about to embark on a self-destructive course to take over the sales department of his father's organization. He had been encouraged by outside professionals. Luckily, the son was able to do some career planning with our industrial psychologist. By having a discussion about expectations for his position and role with his supervisor and the director of sales, the son created a career plan and was able to realize the inappropriateness of his unrealistic expectations. As a result, the son was able to create a realistic career plan that met his goals, the needs of the non-family managers, and his father's ambitions for his son's success.

Senior-generation members of family-owned businesses often have this same issue of entitlement. Being the founder of the company and/or being in the senior generation gives some people a sense of entitlement that allows them to think they should continue to take on the primary responsibility of leadership. This is often at the expense of their younger-generation adult children, who sometimes are in their forties and fifties and still waiting for an opportunity to lead the company.

Clearly, the solution here is to work together to talk about the best interests of the B.O.S.S. and how we can continue to help the B.O.S.S. be successful. When family business constituents have a Common Family Vision™, it alleviates this issue of entitlement and makes it much easier to create succession strategies and solutions that are win-win.

#6: Scarcity

One of the most difficult issues in the context of family business succession planning is the issue of scarcity. What makes it so insidious is the fact that it is invisible because of the underlying assumption of the family that there isn't enough to go around. It often manifests itself in the discussion of money, roles, and power. In a family-owned business, there are two bottom lines: The first is the standard financial one, and the second is the more invisible, emotional one. It is the lack of expression of appreciation, recognition, and love that is the underlying problem with emotional scarcity.

There are two things I have found that help with the issue of scarcity. The first is having family members talk directly about what they expect from one another. This relates to the number one issue, which I will address later. The second has to do with assisting clients to empower themselves to achieve their fullest potential—whether it is inside or outside the family business. In doing so, they begin to understand the sense of abundance that exists in the world for all of us. A resource I have found to be particularly helpful to clients over the last eight years is the Empowerment Workshop offered by Gayle Straub and David Gershon.[iii] Clients who have participated in this come away with a sense of abundance that allows them not only to be fulfilled but also to talk more directly about their emotional expectations from their families.

#5: History

History is a big factor in all families, and it is certainly true in the context of family-owned businesses. A book on families entitled *The Way We Never Were* by Stephanie Coontz[iv] captures the essence of the concern about history. Although family history generally includes difficulties, we go out of our way to talk only about the good things. We mistakenly try to protect our children from our experiences in our own families of origin. Overlooking history is a major factor in family-owned businesses that are having a hard time creating their futures. Danish philosopher Soren Kierkegaard has been quoted as saying, "Life can only be understood backwards, but it must be lived forwards." Therefore, the full celebration of history is essential for continued family business success. In terms of my experience with clients, not only do they not celebrate their histories, but they also often take the positive aspects of their histories for granted and do not celebrate those, either.

The lesson is admirably portrayed in the movie, *Zorba the Greek*. I see it as a family business tale about an adult son who inherits a mine in Crete. On the way to visit his new mine, the son meets Zorba, a roustabout who cons the son into hiring him to run the mine. As they journey to Crete, the son asks Zorba, "Are you married?" Zorba answers: "Am I not a man? I have a wife, the kids, the house—the full catastrophe."

In the story, the mine turns out to be one catastrophe after another. To the son's dismay, Zorba dances and celebrates the catastrophes and embraces life and all it holds. The film's closing line is uttered by the son, "Zorba, will you teach me how to dance?" It captures in metaphor a business-family dilemma, "Would you teach me how to embrace life?"

Jon Kabat-Zinn, founder of the Pain & Stress Reduction Clinic at the University of Massachusetts, teaches patients to embrace the pain. He uses this concept in the title of his book, *Full Catastrophe Living.*[v] In family businesses, the paradox is that in order to go forward, you must embrace the loss. As family-owned businesses are able to celebrate and embrace all that life has to offer, they open the door to the future.

The importance of embracing history is what I call the paradox of change. The paradox is that when you can accept and embrace all of the difficult things in your life, you are then free to go forward and create a new beginning.

#4: Other-oriented regarding change
Change is one of the most difficult aspects of life for all of us. My experience has been that even when the change is positive, it is still difficult. In the context of family-owned businesses, it is not unusual for people to expect others to change in order for something good to occur. But this expectation is a formula for disaster.

Whenever I tell the story of the young man and his statement about overlapping family and business circles at seminars, the participants always laugh. It is quite an amusing story, but I believe it demonstrates the issue of being other-oriented regarding change. The overlap of circles, which is an organizational problem in the context of family-owned businesses, is experienced by family business participants as an interpersonal issue. As a result, they often blame one another and expect the others to change.

The solution is taking responsibility for what we successfully contribute to the family business, as well as recognizing our contribution to the problem. One of the major challenges in succession planning and family-owned businesses is helping clients take full responsibility.

#3: Control
Control is a major issue in the context of succession planning in family-owned businesses. The issue of control, which is the very thing that makes owner-entrepreneurs successful, is also their Achilles' heel. At seminars I often cite the late Curt Carlson, Minnesota's most famous and successful entrepreneur, as an example of this. His struggle with the issue of control and the number of different people he had in his organization as potential successors was chronicled in the media very effectively. The reality is that it is not only the entrepreneurs but also the family as a whole who have to deal with the issue; it is about change. As I mentioned earlier, change is difficult even when it is positive. It is a major issue for an entrepreneur who

has spent the majority of his or her life closely involved with the family business.

In preparation for a recent presentation on aging and entrepreneurs, I began to realize that almost all of my clients were senior citizens. In thinking through the presentation, I began to realize how treacherous the succession planning process is, insofar as it causes entrepreneurs to think that people are trying to change them and take away their companies. Subsequently, I have been able to realize and work with entrepreneurs to help them develop a new dream. Entrepreneurs are driven by their dreams. Since it is not possible to change or control entrepreneurs, it does not make sense to continue to fight that battle. On the other hand, it is possible and realistic to assist entrepreneurs and their families in developing new dreams in relation to their families, their businesses, their communities, their leisure time, and their philanthropy as a way to effectively deal with the issue of control.

#2: Lack of forgiveness

In the family businesses I have worked with over the past thirty-plus years where there has been a breakdown in family relationships, lack of forgiveness is right at the top of the list of things that get in the way. It is impossible to go through life and be involved in a family business without inadvertently stepping on one another's toes. I have observed that the families that don't have the capacity to forgive one another for their transgressions clearly have a hard time being in business together. To bridge this gap successfully, I have generally used and drawn upon my clients' religious backgrounds, since most religions have a philosophy of forgiveness that is often helpful. I also suggest that clients read the aforementioned *A Little Book of Forgiveness*.[vi] It helps clients change their perspective about forgiving one another, and sometimes even themselves.

#1: Lack of appreciation and recognition

Based on my experience with family-owned businesses, the number one obstacle is lack of appreciation, recognition, and love. When I read in the press about family business catastrophes, as well as review in my mind where my own clients' breakdowns occur, lack of appreciation is often at the root. The senior generation desperately wants this from their adult children, but they will deny to their dying day the fact that they want it and need it. At the same time, I have had clients who say, "What I really want is a little love around here."

Another story I tell at seminars is about Bud Grant, a Minnesota icon and former coach of the Minnesota Vikings. In his 1994 acceptance speech into the Pro Football Hall of Fame in Canton, Ohio, he expressed appreciation for his success to everyone he could think of. He stood there, rather uncharacteristically, in a pastel sport coat wearing large sunglasses. He indicated that if his dad were there at the ceremony, he would have said, "You done good, kid!" At this point, he began to choke up with tears. There is absolutely nothing wrong with the fact that he was expressing such emotion on this wonderful occasion, but the fact is that the then almost-seventy-year-old man was still looking for appreciation and recognition from his father, who I assume was long deceased.

It is the same issue for the younger-generation adult children. They are still looking to be recognized by their parents for their accomplishments and uniqueness. Not feeling recognized and appreciated underlies many of the problems in family-owned businesses.

Joseph Jaworski, in his book *Synchronicity: The Inner Path of Leadership*,[vii] mentions his own experiences with his famous father, Leon Jaworski, who was a prosecuting attorney for the Watergate trial and the Nuremberg trials. As a result of his father's army experience, Joseph refers to his father endearingly as "the Colonel." One day, he was journaling and realized that he had some animosity toward his father. He went to his father at their ranch, and here is his description of what transpired:

> *"Colonel, I don't think you've ever told me you love me. I believe you do love me, but why haven't you told me so?"*
>
> *He just kept quiet. He didn't know what to say. After a while he looked down and said, "Well, you know I love you."*

And I said, "Well, why can't you tell me?"

He said, "I've always loved you, and you know I have. You know I love you."

I said, "I don't know it, and it hurts that you never told me so."

I believe this exchange pointedly describes the dynamic that often occurs in family-owned businesses. There is an implicit assumption that people are loved, but the fact that it is rarely, if ever, expressed is often an obstacle.

The solution lies in teaching family members how to talk about their expectations of one another in an emotional sense and to express appreciation, recognition, and love. Many families have a hard time doing this and take it for granted. From my experience, most families across the board need to learn that the emotional bottom line in family-owned businesses is just as important, if not more important, than the financial bottom line. Appreciation, recognition, and love need to be expressed on a regular basis.

Over the years, I have come to realize the importance of planning for success. As a result, it is critically important to incorporate a plan that addresses these obstacles. Addressing them proactively and in a positive way can only enhance a family business's opportunity for continued success and prosperity—both financially and emotionally.

My first lessons on the importance of planning came when I was a junior in high school and working for Knowlan's, a family-owned grocery store in Saint Paul, Minnesota. Bill Knowlan, the oldest of the four siblings who owned the company, was the president. Bill was a prisoner of war and survivor during World War II. He always spoke in riddles and was quite a jocular man. One day when I was stamping No. 303 tins of peas and placing them on the shelves, Bill came down the aisle and asked me, "What's your plan?" I was exasperated with his question and responded, "I don't have a plan. I'm busy putting peas on the shelf!" Bill responded, "A plan that isn't working is better than no plan at all." Then Bill walked away from me, and I thought, what a dumb thing to say. But I have used it during my entire career. You can never create a plan in the midst of a crisis.

Inside-Out Succession Planning™

Only about one in three first-generation family-owned businesses successfully transfer to the children, and a quarter of those businesses fail to transition to a third generation. Why such dismal results?

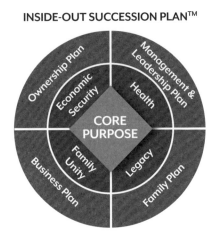

INSIDE-OUT SUCCESSION PLAN™

In my experience, it's because the founder did not adequately plan for succession. The succession program was not anchored by a clear "inside-out" reason.

Applying a Model

I coined the concept of Inside-Out Succession Planning™ from the realization that owner-entrepreneurs must first decide why to develop a succession plan. They must ask and answer, "What is my core purpose?" Only then can a plan truly succeed.

What is that core purpose? Why would an entrepreneur plan for succession? Age? Family pressure? The feeling that it's time to pass the baton? Yes . . . and no.

Yes, there can be different core purposes. They represent the inside ring of the model and include economic security, health, family unity, and legacy. These four core purposes adequately identify the range of motivations for succession planning, which I will discuss in a moment.

But a core purpose will not produce a successful succession plan as long as it remains vague or undefined, such as, "I'm getting too old for this." The entrepreneur who has a clear purpose is motivated to give direction to the plan. Once motivated, the entrepreneur can integrate that core purpose into the four different, yet related, plans. These four plans are the perimeter of the Inside-Out Succession Plan™ model.

Missing the Bull's-Eye

The core purpose is the bull's-eye to aim for and hit. Knowing the core purpose is the entrepreneur's critical first step in developing a succession plan.

I believe that many business families confuse succession planning with ownership planning. Ownership planning is just one of the four processes at the perimeter of the Inside-Out Succession Plan™ model. Entrepreneurs go directly to an ownership plan because it is a common myth in family-business circles that the primary reason for completing ownership and estate planning (their concept of succession planning) is to avoid taxes. So by default, the core purpose for succession planning becomes avoiding taxes.

In my experience, it is not unusual for technical professionals to support this notion. They plan from the perimeter, or the outside-in, using one of the areas depicted on the outer ring of the model.

When tax planning and tax savings replace the core purpose, a tax-driven program can create problems for the family. I frequently see ownership of stock gifted prematurely to younger-generation adult children, only to have those young adults say that they want to be bought out when it comes time to plan for succession.

That's just one example of why the entrepreneur must first have a clear, underlying core purpose that drives succession planning. Let's look more closely at these four core purposes.

1. Economic security

Owner-entrepreneurs who are in their sixties and seventies are often quite aware of the need for a financial exit strategy that guarantees their lifestyle. For years they put everything into the businesses they created, and now they need concrete assurance that they can be sustained without putting their business or themselves at risk. Developing a financial exit strategy is critical for a family business. Economic security can be a major factor that includes a financial exit strategy, but succession planning should consider more than tax planning or tax savings.

2. Health

This can be a highly emotional motivation for succession planning because, whether stated or not, owner-entrepreneurs are implying that they are "playing the back nine." This can create fear: fear that they have to let go, fear that they are being forced out, and even fear by others that their loss of leadership could harm the company.

To help overcome these fears, I developed a process called the Last Challenge of Entrepreneurship™. Essentially it means that entrepreneurs need not leave their companies. Instead, they need to change their job descriptions so they become designers and champions, along with their adult children, of the new ownership and leadership arrangement for their business. They are not "promoted out" but rather "promoting the outcome."

3. Legacy

There comes a time in almost everyone's life when a person wonders, or at least thinks about, whether he or she has made a difference in the world. It's as natural as aging and doubly likely for individuals who started and sustained their own successful businesses. The legacy you leave behind includes both the financial aspects of legacy and nonfinancial ones, such as family values, heritage, service, and philanthropy.

This also implies another side of legacy: how we want to be remembered. When most entrepreneurs contemplate retirement, they begin to wonder whether others in the family appreciate what they, as business founders, have done for them.

Most entrepreneurs will deny it, saying they do not have concerns about getting that kind of validation from their families. As a family-business consultant with a psychology background, I can state with confidence that this is a deep, significant, and common desire to consider candidly when determining a core purpose for succession planning. Incidentally, this is also what younger-generation adult children are looking for—parental approval and appreciation for joining the family business.

4. Family unity

No entrepreneur wants his or her family torn apart by business or financial differences. So to preserve family relationships, many families mistakenly avoid talking about their differences (à la Hubler's Speck of Dust Theory™). Yet by not discussing these issues, they inadvertently create the very pile of dust they are trying to avoid. Thus, the core purpose of maintaining family unity could become a key driver for family-business succession planning.

Powering Purpose

An entrepreneur needs to determine what core purpose is his or her motivating reason for creating a succession plan. Is it economic security? Health? Legacy? Family unity? Some combination?

Once that decision is made, the entrepreneur becomes the architect for building the succession plan. And with the involvement of adult children, the transfer of the company becomes an embracing, thoughtful process with a clear and successful outcome.

The Four Essential Plans

There are four different, but interrelated, plans or processes that should be drawn into a complete succession plan. Three of the four plans are directly for the business: the ownership plan, the management and leadership plan, and the business plan. The fourth, the family plan, defines how the family can be a family without the undue influence of the business.

All of the plans are driven by the entrepreneur's core purpose that motivates the reason for the succession. Determining that core will drive decision-making in creating the Four Essential Plans.

1. Ownership

As I stated previously, ownership plans should consider more than just how to save taxes. Ownership succession (ranked by priority) includes: estate planning, economic security, equitable treatment of adult children, and then minimizing estate taxes.

An ownership plan must reflect the entrepreneur's core purpose, and estate planning is part of that ownership. At its basis, the entrepreneur needs to discuss his or her core purpose and determine if another generation of the family wants to, or even should, own and operate the family business. If this is not discussed and decided, huge complications can arise when adult children do not want to continue in the business or, the reverse, the founder realizes that no one else in the family is currently capable of operating the business.

The ownership plan must include economic security for the senior generation. No succession plan can succeed unless the senior generation's economic security can be guaranteed.

The equitable treatment of the adult children is also a key consideration of ownership planning. It is important to understand that equitable is not the same as equal in the context of ownership succession planning. This can cause emotional and complicated issues, especially when there are adult children who are not active in the business or when the family business is the parents' major asset. As a result, equitable treatment among children requires sophisticated technical planning and delicate discussions within the entire family. As technical professionals, it is our responsibility to encourage suggestions from everyone in the family. The entrepreneurial parents should be given this feedback before any estate plan is finalized.

Minimizing estate taxes becomes important only when it's understood who will operate the business, how economic security for the senior generation can be guaranteed, and how adult children can be equitably treated. Technical professionals can do some of their best work for the company and family when they include the family in the process.

An ownership and estate plan also includes directions concerning governance. All family businesses are legally required to have a board of directors. Generally, most boards are inactive and meet only on an annual basis to fulfill legal requirements. When only the entrepreneur is involved in the business, an annual meeting may work fine. However, when many family members are involved in the business, it is imperative to have an active board of directors that includes outside advisors and members.

Ernesto Poza writes in his book Family Business (3rd ed.)[viii] that family businesses with active boards and outside advisors are more successful than those that don't have these structures in place. When the entrepreneur is succeeded, an active board of directors (or at least outside, expert advisors) is vital to helping develop a new or at least future-forward system.

I have worked with many advisory boards and have seen how they can soften the relationship between an entrepreneur and a son or daughter. Instead of reporting to a parent, adult children are reporting to a board that facilitates the parent-child relationship.

2. Management and leadership
There are several components of a management and leadership plan:

- Career plan for the owner-entrepreneur
- Career and leadership plan for the next generation

- Clear decision-making

- Family Participation Plan™

- Compensation arrangements

- The Last Challenge of Entrepreneurship™

Entrepreneurs must decide what gives personal meaning to their work and use that passion to develop a plan for their future career. Succession is not necessarily about disappearing from the business; it's about arranging the company's leadership to teach the younger generation about the business and help them acquire the knowledge that develops their personal leadership skills.

Finally, compensation and decision-making are two of the more difficult issues facing family-owned businesses. These issues are qualitative as well as quantitative, and they are instinctive as well as measurable, which can make them difficult to discuss unemotionally. Thus, putting structure and formality into these areas is vital for both the family and the business.

3. Business

A formal business plan is essential when more than one family member works in the business. I often use online resources with clients to begin the strategic planning discussion. I have each family member complete a survey, which gives us an assessment of their perspectives about the company. Then, the family group meets to discuss their individual scores strategically and begin the business planning process.

Business plans are like fingerprints; no two are alike. But more than personally identified, they are also necessary for and descriptive of each business.

4. Family

Going into business with your family involves much more than just creating a business and much more than just maintaining a family. This type of endeavor requires a skilled balancing act between family and business. You must nurture the ability to leave business at work and always work on keeping your family strong. Many family-business owners refer to this as the family plan, or the effort the members of a successful family business put into maintaining the family and the business as separate-but-equal entities. Many times, families will crumble even as the business thrives, which is just as unhealthy as allowing the business to fold because of family dynamics. It's critically important to build the emotional equity of the family while you're simultaneously building the equity of the business.

The Family Meeting

Too often, family business owners put far too much emphasis on the business, believing they are working to provide for their family now and in the future. However, this allows for a breakdown in communication, which can result in divorce and estrangement, even when the business thrives. The breakdown in communication can multiply exponentially and create unfathomable issues that lead to resentment and pure hatred at times. This is why prioritizing the family meeting is essential for family-owned businesses, as I've noted previously. The concept of like-minded people meeting together to work toward common goals is an age-old concept that can be easily brought into the world of family business.

Build Your Family's Emotional Equity

Life happens. Business happens. Often, decisions in life and business are made that are not popular but are best for the people involved on most levels. When this occurs in business, you can typically go home and separate yourself from your business. You have a chance to digest and think about the effects of those decisions. As a result, your business can grow, and you can maintain a level of contentment both in and out of work.

However, when you are involved in a family business, you cannot often step away and separate yourself from work. Without a family plan, you lose your family's emotional equity as a result of not being able to compartmentalize your work and home life successfully. As a result, the business may build equity and thrive, but the family will fall apart. Business and financial differences will always eventually erode family relationships unless the family makes a commitment to simultaneously build the equity of their family. This defeats the point of maintaining a family business. The idea of a family business is to strengthen your family both emotionally and financially. Otherwise, it is best just to have a business and keep your family separate. However, if you are willing to work on your family as well as your business, properly managing a family business can help your family appreciate one another and maintain wealth, as well.

The key is understanding that family and family business must be in sync with each other to be successful. Resentment, loss of family ties, and a general breakdown of communication will hurt the family, of course. But it can also harm the business, as well, complicating the succession plan and inner workings of the business.

Put It All Together

Think of the Inside-Out Succession Plan™ model as a kind of succession-planning combination lock. The motivations spin around the core purpose to help the entrepreneur dial direction into succession plan thinking. Then the entrepreneur aligns his or her core motivators to each of the four planning processes to lock in a truly successful outcome. The succession plan is secure when all the tumblers line up to the benefit, interests, and capabilities of everyone in the family and across the business.

Granted, that's no small challenge. But it is certainly attainable and worth doing for the good of the business and the joy of the family.

Perpetuating the Family Business

A most challenging aspect of entrepreneurship has nothing to do with who started or maintains the family business, yet it has everything to do with perpetuating it. That challenge is to do all that's required to pass the company on to the next generation.

Previously, I discussed the entrepreneur's responsibilities to create a plan for succession and the next generation. Over the past thirty years I have had many clients who did the technical things: created an ownership plan, formalized an estate plan, and engaged with their family to perpetuate their business legacy. Unfortunately, in some cases, by the time all that was done, the entrepreneur was burned out. He or she had exhausted the energy and desire, and lacked the skills to devote to training and developing the business family's next generation of leaders. A decision had been made to keep the company in the family, but the retiring generation was totally at sea about how to make that happen with their children. While the situation can be frustrating, good results are vital if you are to successfully pass the business baton to the next generation.

A common interim solution is to hire a non-family person as president to run the company and train new family leaders. Many business executives are looking for such an assignment. The trick is to find one suited for your family and company. Here are some tips to help you bridge the gap:

- Look for a person with a proven track record of business growth and success; ask for a bio or other proof of competence.

- Determine that he or she has the skills and temperament to train and mentor; if possible, talk to individuals who have had them as a mentor.

- Determine how well the prospective candidate fits into your business family culture. For example, someone from large, public corporations may not comfortably fit in a small, family work culture.

- Discuss mutual expectations with the candidate to clarify what success looks like. Include in these discussions your expectations for the next-generation leaders.

- Thoroughly explain the family's values, what you expect to see perpetuated in the company, and how the new non-family president can provide leadership.

- Set clear, formal boundaries for the working relationship that will exist between the entrepreneur and the non-family president. Write those rules down.
- Also, write down expectations for company performance. I suggest that the entrepreneur have regular meetings with the non-family president to stay informed about progress.

Beyond an interim non-family president, an active board of directors can enormously benefit the entrepreneur in managing the leadership transition and training the second generation. A strong, competent board can make it easier for both the entrepreneur and a non-family president who reports to the board. An engaged board of directors can broaden the entrepreneur's perspective, reflect company/family history, amplify objectivity, and enhance discussions about any potential shortcomings discovered in the next generation.

Prepare an employment agreement to memorialize the employment expectations for the non-family president. The agreement protects everyone involved and supports the president's ability to monitor new family leaders and hold them accountable. Consult with your attorney to help develop such a document that formalizes the expectations necessary for the continued successful operation of your family business.

Business families are complex entities because they combine so many unusual characteristics—both expressed and unexpressed. This does not mean that an "outsider" is difficult to find or may be challenged to coach the incoming generation. In fact, the right candidate can simultaneously relieve the entrepreneur's stress and launch the family business legacy into a strong future.

Intellectual Property and Succession Planning

Many conflicts can erode family relationships in a family-owned business: succession, ownership, estate management, leadership, retirement, perceived fairness, and more. But one of the most unique and damaging conflicts can be the disagreement over intellectual property. "Intellectual Property and Succession Planning" describes what would seem to be a straightforward process. But those two word pairs can hide a maze of misunderstanding, confusion, and heartache.

Intellectual property can mark a point at which the family, the business, entrepreneurialism, patents, and copyrights may overlap so much that no one clearly recognizes boundaries, sensitivities, or direction. Past and future collide in a fight for the fuzzy present. I have seen it create havoc in personal relationships, tear apart family bonds, and destroy business possibilities. It can devastate a loving family and its thriving business.

FROM THE CASE STUDY FILES: UNCLE JOE AND BRUCE

When I became involved as a family business consultant, Joe and his nephew Bruce were in the middle of a dreadful succession planning ordeal. The typical business-family issues of ownership, estate, and leadership were compounded by a painful history and intellectual property concerns.

The painful history began thirty years earlier when Bruce was ten years old. Both of Bruce's parents (Joe's brother and sister-in-law) were killed in an airplane crash. At the time of the tragedy, Joe had left the family's construction business and started one of his own, eventually bringing in his two sons, Bruce's cousins. (I know this is complicated, feel free to read that sentence again!)

With both parents deceased, Uncle Joe invited ten-year-old Bruce into his family. Everyone did their best to make Bruce feel welcome and part of the family, as all three boys were about the same age.

Joe's two sons attended college and returned to join their father's business. Bruce also graduated from college but went his own way, working at various marketing positions and exploring his interests. After several years he moved back to his hometown.

During that time, tensions rose between Joe and his two biological sons over their construction company. Their working relationship had deteriorated over differences about workload, roles, responsibilities, and decision-making.

Joe, an engineer, had also created an invention. He had consulted an attorney and obtained patent protection for his idea. He could see the potential source of revenue and did his best to protect his patent and revenue stream, but he had done very little else with his idea. It was essentially only potential, though Joe had ideas and future plans for this separate company.

Tensions grew within Joe's construction company. His two talented sons finally said either he would leave the family business or they would. Reluctantly, Joe left. He was phased out of his own construction business.

Having come back home, Bruce became interested in his Uncle Joe's patented invention and began collaborating with him on it. Bruce conducted marketing surveys, attended trade shows, and determined that there was an opportunity for a viable business selling the invention. Initially, Bruce and Joe got along well, but as this separate business grew, Bruce wanted more control. Bruce pressured his uncle for a succession plan that would give him future controlling interest in the company and, in the meantime, allow him to continue to make major leadership decisions.

Joe was in his early seventies but balked at creating a succession plan. He was not ready to retire. Bruce realized that if he grew the company, it would be more expensive for him to buy it. Plus, Joe owned the patent that was the basis of the company's success. This was the state of the dreadful succession-planning ordeal that I was brought in to fix.

I talked with Joe and Bruce. I interviewed family members who were engaged in but not part of their business. I came to recognize that neither Joe nor Bruce was a good communicator. Each could not respect the other's perspective. Uncle Joe did not understand Bruce's concern about the expense of buying the company and controlling his own destiny. Bruce could not appreciate Joe's need for security, protection of the patent, and feeling relevant in the company.

Despite the help of their professional advisor and their own best efforts, Joe and Bruce were deadlocked. No formal agreements existed between them. Unfortunately, this is not unusual in many family businesses. As I've previously noted, written agreements and formal structure are commonly ignored by relatives who are in business together. In fact, formalities such as this may be viewed with mistrust. Merely bringing them up can trigger hurt feelings.

Unresolved emotional issues added to the complexity between Joe and Bruce as they tried to resolve patent and succession issues. Bruce had never expressed his own hurt feelings over how his parents' property and family heirlooms were dispersed at the time of their death; he was ten, and Joe and his family never consulted him about their family treasures.

Joe, on the other hand, felt unappreciated for taking Bruce into his family. The hurts were deep and unspoken on both sides.

SOLUTION

To begin the healing, I suggested the Family Forgiveness Ritual™. The entire family participated, including Joe and his wife, his adult children and their spouses, and Bruce and his spouse. The emotional relief for the family was spectacular. The entire family joined together to create a new beginning. The Family Forgiveness Ritual™ opened the emotional door and established an openness and positive foundation for productive business discussions.

Working together with love and respect for one another, the family resolved their business issues regarding ownership, leadership, and the patent. But it took time and many meetings. Joe eventually sold his share of the business to Bruce. Joe retained patent ownership until his death and then the patent transferred to Bruce.

The family learned the hard lessons:

- Many, if not most, technical issues can be minimized by setting clear ground rules or expectations when the business is begun.

- Understand and record the plan for future ownership or potential licensing and/or future sale of a patent.

- Conduct regular family meetings to uncover, discuss, and relieve emotional issues that can provoke the best of families and their business.

In these areas and more, professional advisors can offer guidance and leadership to help a business family avoid the intellectual property maze that is often emotionally charged, as well as technically complex.

Intellectual property law firms and professional services can help you:

- Determine the patentability of an invention

- Prepare, file, and prosecute patent applications in the United States and internationally

- Investigate, defend, and prosecute claims of infringement

- Enforce patent rights through litigation or alternative dispute resolution (ADR)

- License, police, and manage patent portfolios

- Oversee the acquisition and sale of patented technology

A Special Note about Female Entrepreneurs

Women's roles in family businesses have been historically underrated, especially with regard to succession planning. But the truth is, there are myriad examples of spouses stepping in after an entrepreneurial husband has died and running the business successfully. There are also cases where a husband and wife team created the business together, and the wife carries on quite successfully after her husband dies, as well as numerous instances where women entrepreneurs start up and run very successful companies.

Betty Novak is a classic example of a women entrepreneur, who together with her husband, Ken, ran their family business. Betty focused on the administrative functions, but more importantly, she ran the sales and marketing division that was the heart and soul of the business. Ken was involved with the engineering and design work, but it was really Betty's leadership that fueled the success of their company.

As a female entrepreneur, Betty had no formal training in business, but she grew with the business primarily because of her exceptional people and relationship skills with customers and employees. She was effective in sales and marketing, and because of her impressive technical, mathematical, and analytical skills, she was the primary estimator for the company and bid on projects quite successfully. Betty contributed all of these talents, while maintaining her role as wife and mother.

Betty and Ken's son and son-in-law, both of whom worked in the business, were being groomed to take over when Ken was diagnosed with Alzheimer's disease. During the initial stages of Ken's illness, Betty continued to work full time while simultaneously being Ken's main caregiver. Her children supported Betty's continued involvement in the business, and they helped provide care for their father on the home front.

The company's succession plan provided a framework for Betty to work as long as she could—and when the time came for her to be more involved with Ken's care, she would cut back and work with a non-family manager to lead the company and mentor her son and son-in-law.

Karen Hanson, another successful entrepreneur, inherited the family construction business when her husband, Richard, died unexpectedly of a heart attack. Karen's original career was in elementary education, and as her three sons were born, she eventually left teaching to become a full-time mom. After Richard's death, Karen took over leadership of the company despite lacking formal business training and knowledge of the construction business. In addition, Richard owned and managed a working ranch, and Karen supervised the ranch manager and made major contributions to decision-making, planning, and budgeting for the ranch.

Karen's major challenge was managing her three sons, all of whom worked in the company, while simultaneously managing their collective grief over Richard's death—a lot for anyone to handle! Karen then successfully led the succession planning process and, with assistance from an outside resource, was able to identify which roles and responsibilities best fit her sons' abilities and create a business plan that solidified the continued growth and success of their construction business.

One of my former clients owned a major manufacturing company that supplied the construction industry. He created a succession plan in which he chose his daughter, Sharon, as successor and leader of the third-generation company. Although she was succeeding in a male-dominated industry, the thought of having a daughter/sister at the helm was not initially well-received by the male-dominated family. Sharon was chosen after she successfully completed a leadership assessment and after several family discussions. Fast-forward twenty years, and Sharon has successfully grown the company, retired, and passed company leadership onto the fourth-generation—and she continues to be active in the company as the chair of the board.

Preparing for the Unthinkable: Loss of the Entrepreneur

No one expects to die prematurely. After all, when wouldn't anyone consider the death of a loved one to be premature? In a family business, the entrepreneur's unexpected death or incapacitation opens a fissure in the business and in the family—double devastation.

Families who own a business typically have no time or inclination to prepare "early" for the loss of the entrepreneur, who is often the head of both the business and the family. There is often no succession plan in place, especially when the entrepreneur is "robust" regardless of age, and certainly no one is prepared for the emotional tsunami and financial impact of such overwhelming loss.

I cannot imagine the doubling of emotional and commercial impact, but several of my clients have suffered such crushing events. I selected three to illustrate strikingly different reactions that can occur after such a loss: the Horwaths, the Watsons, and the Andersons. Each suffered the premature loss of the family-business owner/entrepreneur. Each coped naturally, yet the way in which each business family responded provides valuable lessons on how better to prepare for the unthinkable.

FROM THE CASE STUDY FILES: THE HORWATH FAMILY

Mr. Horwath, father and entrepreneur, was the heart and soul of an auto company and larger than life. His long-established business relationships and historic marketplace savvy directed the company's success. Suddenly, he was gone.

His two sons vied for his chair and position in the family. Each believed in his own capacity to move the company forward. Each saw it as survival, not mean-spiritedness. Their competition caught their mother, who now owned the company, between two sons she loved.

The turmoil in the company inhibited the family's natural grieving process and interfered with succession planning in the company.

Under the circumstances, typical approaches to family business intervention languished. Nothing was resolved in family meetings to discuss the loss of the father, in leadership assessments to determine the more qualified son to head the business, or in discussions about creating a board of directors. Horwath family members were simply unable or unwilling to understand the impact of their loss and acknowledge those feelings.

Family dynamics, as well as business disruptions, add special stresses to family businesses. One would think that the intimacy of a family in business together would rally rather than isolate family members. In my experience, the opposite often happens: Family members avoid the topic, act as if nothing has changed emotionally, and maintain isolated individual business viewpoints. The family is no longer a team. They are unable to share their loss and work through feelings of vulnerability.

WHEN GRIEVING EVOLVES INTO COMPETITION

Unfortunately, many of the emotional themes I presented to the Horwath family seemed extraneous or even impertinent and did not seem relevant to the family and company's culture. The family did not want to talk about their feelings. The grieving process instead manifested in the sons' competition for the father's role. It has taken many years for them to work through their emotional responses to their father's death.

The brothers continue to work on the strategic issues of the company. The process has helped them be more collaborative, though they continue to wrestle with the challenge of creating a board involving outside advisors. The company has changed from their father's aggressive on-the-fly business approach to one that is much more conservative and traditional, as the sons could not rely on their father's reputation and business contacts. Essentially, the sons needed to develop a new marketing strategy but were unable to understand the gap between their father's philosophy of success and what the company needed in order to prosper.

A powerful lesson in this case is to not grieve alone. No matter how stoic one may be, each individual grieves, which makes it essential to share grief with other family members. It is altogether different from merely mentioning it to colleagues or friends. Sharing this experience with others in the family brings them closer together and expedites healing. Making grief part of family meetings allows you to share loving memories of the entrepreneur that also support understanding and health. At the same time, sharing in a family meeting gives family members opportunities to ask one another what support they need. It shares and speaks to grief and doesn't just assume it.

FROM THE CASE STUDY FILES: THE WATSON FAMILY

The Watson father/entrepreneur knew he was going to die of cancer. He prepared. He worked with an attorney to create a trust that would own the family real estate business for the benefit of his wife and their four children. But the trust was also created to influence events after his death. In part, it kept his wife out of the business, and it addressed the fact that the four inexperienced children were not ready to take over the company. In his mind, he was planning for a stable succession of leadership.

As the father drew closer to his death, he met with his advisors and appointed his wife and attorney as trustees. They formed a board of directors that included his wife, attorney, financial advisor, the company's accountant, his oldest son, and the non-family president of the company. On the surface, one would think the plan was well-considered and carefully planned. Then reality entered in.

After the elder Watson died, his wife chafed under the restrictions of the trust. She thought she should control the business. She resented what she believed were her late husband's attempts to control her. This situation might have been avoided if family meetings had been held so that the entire family, including the father/entrepreneur, could share his vision of what new roles and changes would help accommodate a new configuration of the family business.

Another great resource for aiding the transition of control would have been having a board of directors and outside advisory members already in place. The board could have offered key assistance during the critical transfer period and helped create interim leadership. The board could also have helped hire and select a replacement president for the company.

A FAMILY PARTICIPATION PLAN™

A Family Participation Plan™ also would have helped the Watson family determine new roles, affirm changed relationships, recognize the next generation, and address standards, expectations, and compensations for family members working in the company.

As it stands, the Watson widow continues to lobby for control of the company even though she owns no stock and is just one of several trust beneficiaries. She comes to the company daily, which causes conflict with the non-family president. My own assurances to professionalize the board and create some distance between the president and the widow has offered some relief. We began regular monthly meetings to inform the Watson widow about the success of the company and review monthly financials to assure her the company is well run. In addition, the widow has arranged to have one son mentored to be the future company president. The board is now reorganized and more professional, and it created a search committee that selected four independent outside members.

The Anderson family father/entrepreneur recruited his son, who was already working successfully in another city at a parallel business, to join the family construction business. He and his son were at odds from the beginning. The son was ambitious and wanted to grow the business. The father, in his day, was an aggressive entrepreneur, but as he grew older became more risk-averse. Risk turned from a business issue into a father-son conflict. Their once-close relationship was strained and deteriorating rapidly.

I was asked to address the deterioration of their relationship and help them resolve their differences. I suggested a joint approach that respected both father's and son's visions for the company's future growth. In those frank, respectful, coached discussions they developed an entirely new market for their business that both equally endorsed.

Over the next three years, father and son implemented many of my business recommendations. One was that they create a board of directors with outside advisors. This was no easy task. After numerous discussions for more than a year, the board was finalized. Despite the entrepreneur's initial reluctance, he became a full participant in selecting four outstanding advisory members who brought industry experience and added value to the board. Two years after the board was finalized, the father died unexpectedly.

All the work, discussion, and preparation father and son had done together kept the family and the business on solid ground. During the preceding three years, the family had developed the business plan, created an active board of directors with advisory members, and completed leadership training for the son. In addition, the widow, who had her husband's power of attorney, was able to complete the gifting of company stock to the adult children and grandchildren, thus taking advantage of current tax exemptions.

The son, who became company president before his father's death, successfully leads the business. He uses the board as a guide to streamline the company for efficiencies, financial savings, and profitability.

On the business side, it is important not only to solidify company leadership, but also to reach out to all employees. A family business is like a family in many ways. As a result, acknowledge the emotional loss for employees and assure them of the family's continued commitment to them and the company. The family may decide to hold company-wide or department meetings to share the impact of the loss with employees.

It is also important to reach out to the customers in a timely manner and reassure them about the company's stability and the family's commitment to the future. Financial partners, bankers, and other professional advisors should also be quickly included in plans for the future.

On the emotional side, the Anderson family continues to grieve the loss of the entrepreneur. But it is shared grief. The family has come together because of this major, sad event and is now even closer.

The Anderson family joined with the community to honor the father's life and legacy in a memorial ceremony. It was not only a tribute to the entrepreneur, but it also contributed to the healing process for the community as well as the family. The son is currently working with a family historian to capture family histories that honor his father and perpetuate his legacy for future generations.

The lesson teaches how important it is to continue emotional support and share experiences for the long haul. Healing does not happen overnight, and it usually takes longer if feelings are suppressed and business preparations are delayed.

My advice for any family, especially those working together in business, is an ageless oath with a twist: Be prepared emotionally, as well as practically. At every opportunity, contribute to the common good of your family out of your generosity, love, sense of abundance, and trust. Make it your lifestyle and conscious attitude. It will support everyone during any unforeseen event, especially if a leader and loved one is taken from you.

The Last Challenge of Entrepreneurship™

Entrepreneurs are driven by their dreams, for they are the fuel that drives business growth and success. But the Last Challenge of Entrepreneurship™ lies in developing a new dream for this next phase of life, and this can be the greatest challenge of all. Entrepreneurs don't have to leave their companies and retire, but they do have to change their job descriptions and become the architects and designers of the new ownership and management systems of their companies. We develop career/leadership plans for the younger generation; at the same time, we need to develop Life Career Plans™.

Letting go and saying goodbye to your role in the company is a terribly difficult family business issue. This and the other challenges that an entrepreneur must face before moving onto the next phase of life might seem overwhelming, but over the years I have compiled a checklist (see Appendix, page 191) for my clients to use during the transition.

Because letting go is such a challenge, it contributes significantly to the fact that nearly three-quarters (seventy percent) of families fail to maintain their business into the second generation.[ix] Many blame mom or dad for not letting go, but indeed the whole family resists change and cannot let go.

Emotional and career issues are at stake. More subtly, perhaps, there is the resonance of the big letting go—death—that subconsciously entwines with giving up the management reins. Often the entire family avoids the discussion to keep from creating an "emotional backwash," as one client recently put it.

As I've already pointed out, most senior-generation entrepreneurs will forever deny that they need other members of their families to appreciate their efforts. Yet virtually all want validation from their adult children. Aging entrepreneurs in particular will ask themselves: "Have I made a difference? Has my life meant something?"

Certainly adult children appreciate their parents, but they usually fail to express that appreciation. In my experience, the hurt of feeling unappreciated or taken for granted causes most of the tension in family business succession planning. The entrepreneur wants to be appreciated and validated for what he or she has accomplished. Conversely, validation is exactly what the adult children want from their parents. All sides feel slighted.

The loss of significance is another emotional factor hindering the succession planning process. Successful adults take significance for granted because it is natural to feel worthy during one's working life. However, many retirees have told me their sense of being significant critically diminished once they stopped working.

Once the center of everything in his company, a recently retired entrepreneur told me he worked hard his entire life to build a successful company. At age sixty-seven, he had decided now was the time to bring his family together to discuss his plans for the future and how he envisioned things for both the company and the family. As part of his presentation, the entrepreneur mentioned some of the financial details and how each of the adult children would benefit. He was talking about significant amounts of money and was expecting a lot of validation and appreciation for his efforts.

To the contrary, what occurred was the resurrection of some old, unresolved hurts that gradually evolved into a family fight. What the entrepreneur hoped would be a wonderful family meeting where the children could understand what he had created for them instead turned out to be a nightmare.

The emotional factors that affect succession are powerful: fear of letting go and the need to feel appreciated and remain significant. To answer these Last Challenges of Entrepreneurship™ is not difficult when business family members and entrepreneurs systematically address these concerns. First, it must be acknowledged that they are issues for the entire family to address—not just the mother or father who started the company.

I usually begin the process by helping the entrepreneur shape a plan for his or her career in a manner that recognizes the needs of the family, the company, and the non-family employees. (Remember helping the B.O.S.S.—Business; Other; Self; and Stakeholders.)

When these constituencies are acknowledged, succession is successful and even joyous. Entrepreneurs don't need to abandon their companies; they simply need to change their job descriptions. This might mean becoming chairman of the board and designing, with the adult children's input, a new leadership system for the company.

(For excellent resources on Life Career Planning™, see Appendix, page 201.)

FROM THE CASE STUDY FILES: JIM AND ROBERT

Consider the tale of Jim, an entrepreneur who started his family business, and Robert, the non-family member Jim hired when he decided to step down from the company. Jim had a son who was not quite ready to take over the business, so he asked Robert to run the company and train his son.

ALL THE RIGHT INTENTIONS

Jim nurtured the company from a garage start-up to an enterprise making $40 million annually. To ensure a smooth transition, Jim met monthly with Robert, his new president, to review the company's performance. At one such meeting, Jim noticed Robert's last item on the agenda: "Jim's Schedule." When they got to it, Robert said, "Jim, if I'm going to be successful around here, you can't be here as much." Shocked, Jim thought: "What will I do? The company is my life." Then he thought about his hobby farm and his boat on Lake Michigan and decided he would be fine; he had plenty to do.

A few months later, the last agenda item was once again "Jim's Schedule." Jim said, "Well, Robert, at least I'm doing a better job of not being around as much." Robert shook his head slowly. Jim's continued presence in the company undermined Robert's leadership. Jim could not, in his mind, "quit" the company.

The decision to step down and retire is one of the hardest decisions a family business entrepreneur ever makes. But entrepreneurs don't have to retire and leave their companies. Instead, they must change their job descriptions. Jim should become the architect and designer of new ownership, management, and leadership systems. He should be the lead family member to organize and build consensus on family values and family philanthropy. He doesn't have to quit; he must lead from a new perspective.

In my thirty years of consulting with family-owned businesses, I have seen many entrepreneurs who failed at the letting go process. The breakdown tends to come from a failure in communication. And how do you replace an entrepreneur? Truthfully, you can't. In all my years of working with family-owned businesses, I have never seen a "replacement entrepreneur." It's an oxymoron, like "jumbo shrimp." But it is possible to develop a system that provides stability and direction for a family business.

An owner-entrepreneur does not have to leave the company for this to happen. He or she needs to change roles and become the designer to help develop the new system for business leadership and governance.

Leadership prepares the next generation
To produce leadership, the entrepreneur must establish a process that helps next-generation adult children maximize the leverage of

their gifts to benefit the company and fulfill themselves. This requires a commitment on the part of both the company and the family to support and develop the younger generation of adults. When more than one adult child is involved, the entrepreneur should establish a leadership team that helps the next generation find an appropriate place in the company, based on their talents. According to Jim Collins' book *Good to Great*,[x] you need to allow the next generation the chance to "find the right seat on the bus."

Governance requires a board of directors

In my experience, owner-entrepreneur companies have a board of directors, but it is usually inactive or, at best, a kitchen cabinet of senior managers, professionals working with the company, friends of the entrepreneur, and sometimes family members.

To meet the Last Challenge of Entrepreneurship™ successfully, a family business needs an active board of directors consisting of either outside advisors or family members. There are good arguments for either, but its purpose is the same: to provide objectivity and strategic wisdom so the business continues to prosper.

In addition, the board of directors can function as an intermediary between the owner-entrepreneur and the younger-generation adult son or daughter who is running the company. As I've noted previously, it is much easier for the company's next-generation president to report to a board rather than to mom or dad.

For the business, a board of directors is good business: Ernesto Poza's research shows that family businesses with active boards of outside advisors are significantly more profitable than family businesses that do not have an active board.

A board needs critical design factors

Several design factors guide the process of developing a board of directors:

- Create a prospectus for prospective board members that describes the company, including an overview of the business, its most important products, the industry, types of customers, size of the company, and the nature of ownership.

- Include a board profile that covers the character of the business, stages of the life cycle of the business, strengths and weaknesses of the business, strategic thrust of the business, and plans for growth and market share development.

Define the purpose of the board with tasks that could include:

- Examining and brainstorming strategic directions in the face of market maturity or intensifying competition.

- Stimulating continued management professionalism and organizational development.

- Helping develop the succession process and supporting successors.

- Counseling spouse and successors if the CEO dies or is severely disabled.

- Encouraging and increasing self-discipline and accountability with the president and across the organization.

- Articulating personal criteria and desired background and personal characteristics of outside advisor members of the board. Most importantly, avoid choosing friends. Instead, select trusted professionals who can add value to the company.

Another aspect of ownership planning is creating an estate plan that corresponds to your plan for the transition of stock to the next generation. The five priorities of estate planning include:

1. A decision about whether there will be another generation of the family who will own and run the company. If the decision is yes, this becomes the key component of the succession-planning process.

2. Economic security for the senior generation. No succession plan will succeed unless the parents' economic security is guaranteed or they retain voting control until they are removed from the personal guarantees.

3. Equitable treatment of the adult children. Often the most challenging aspect of succession planning is the equitable treatment of adult children—those working inside and outside the business. It can be difficult for parents who love their adult children equally to implement transition plans that do not treat them as exact equals.

4. Minimization of estate taxes. After the family clarifies the succession plan, professional advisors can go to work and create the most efficient course of action. It often requires five to ten years to implement the plan, and now is the time to begin.

5. Family awareness of the plan before it is finalized. Using the family meeting format, it is critically important for the parents to review the plan with the entire family prior to its finalization. This allows the adult children to have their input into the plan and allows parents to take their adult children's preferences into consideration before the documents are finalized. Having this discussion will go a long way toward preventing family disharmony and hurt feelings.

Happiness, gratitude, and compassion

Another element of the Last Challenge of Entrepreneurship™ is focusing on service and philanthropy that arises from happiness, gratitude, and compassion. But the greatest significance is not the entrepreneur's act of giving per se, but in leading the family to embrace it. The entrepreneur creates a philanthropic spirit by establishing regular family meetings at which everyone can discuss and evaluate whether the family shares the same values about money and wealth. This is where happiness, gratitude, and compassion come in.

What creates happiness? In *Finding Flow*, Mihaly Csikszentmiha-li[xi] sees three things that create flow or fulfillment in people's lives: work, active leisure time, and relationships. Entrepreneurs certainly recognize how work can help produce a happy life. For full happiness, however, we need to manifest our calling or spiritual gifts—representing the person we are and the passions we carry.

Parker Palmer touches on this same topic in his book *Let Your Life Speak*.[xii] Palmer writes, "Our deepest calling is to grow into our own authentic selfhood." To me, that means discovering your spiritual gifts. Your gift to the future is also to help your children recognize and live their spiritual gifts.

Gratitude is a special gift that stimulates philanthropy. In fact, philanthropy is the antidote to consumption and the thousands of advertisements to buy and consume that experts say our children receive every day. Having regular family meetings focused on philanthropy and getting each member of the family involved at an appropriate age is critical to the development of gratitude.

Educating children about giving: a real-world example
I had just heard Nathan Dungan give a presentation on Share Save Spend, which is described in his book *Prodigal Sons and Material Girls: How Not to Become Your Child's ATM*[xiii]. I was so impressed with his concept and immediately started to think about how I could apply it to my own family. On my next visit to my eldest grandchild, Kailey, who was six years old at the time, I explained to her that there were many children whose families did not have enough money for school supplies, new school clothes, and other items, so I was giving her a "share" check that she could give as a present to her school or church.

Kailey immediately asked, "Does this check take the place of my Christmas presents?"

"No," I said. "You will always receive your Christmas presents, but from now on, you will also receive a share check."

Fast-forward to second grade. Kailey called me and said, "Grandpa, I need some money."

"What for?" I asked.

"I'm in the Heart Association Jump-a-thon." I gave her a contribution, and she said, "That's great, Grandpa, now I have $100."

My granddaughter is already philanthropic, developing positive money memories and, most importantly, gaining a sense of gratitude for her blessings.

Performing acts of service to others is what I call "experiential philanthropy." As C. Michael Thompson observes in his book *The Congruent Life*,[xiv] "Service is on the outside like prayer is on the inside." Many families we work with involve their children at an early age in service projects. One family helps deliver Thanksgiving "Meals on Wheels." Another family hosts a Fourth of July picnic and fireworks celebration for a local children's home. The parents and their adult children, spouses, grandchildren, and friends join in serving at these wonderful events. The parents who organize the events are role models who walk their talk. They are living examples for their children and grandchildren. They are living their legacy.

6

THE SOUL OF FAMILY LEGACY

Everyone must leave something behind when he dies,
my grandfather said. A child or a book or a painting or a house
or a wall built or a pair of shoes made. Or a garden planted.
Something your hand touched some way so your soul has
somewhere to go when you die, and when people look at that tree
or that flower you planted, you're there.

It doesn't matter what you do, he said, so long as you change
something from the way it was before you touched it into
something that's like you after you take your hands away.
The difference between the man who just cuts lawns and a
real gardener is in the touching, he said. The lawn-cutter
might just as well not have been there at all;
the gardener will be there a lifetime.
Ray Bradbury, *Fahrenheit 451*

"Are we being good ancestors?"
Jonas Salk (1914–1995)

Laura Nash and Howard Stevenson, in their *Harvard Business Review* article "Success That Lasts,"[i] observe that we should not wait until we are sixty-five years old to start thinking about our legacy; we should distribute our emotional and physical resources (including happiness, achievement, significance, and legacy) throughout our lives.

A 2005 Allianz American Legacies[ii] study noted that baby boomers and their children agree that nonfinancial items (e.g., family stories, family heritage, family values, and religion) are far more important than the financial aspects of inheritance. Yet the study revealed that less than a third of baby boomers and their adult children are having in-depth, meaningful discussions about legacy and inheritance.

HUBLER'S LEGACY MODEL™

Source: Adapted from the Family Legacy Foundation

Legacy is financial and nonfinancial. I have come to look at legacy as your gift to the future to help others find their own success, and my own Hubler's Legacy Model™ contains five interrelated aspects:

1. **Wealth Care** — money and property
2. **Heritage** — history and ancestry
3. **Family/Self** — loving and caring
4. **Business Legacy** — succession plan
5. **Community** — service and philanthropy

Fine-tuning a legacy requires implementing all five aspects of the model.

It's important to capture stories that relate to family and history, and to consciously voice life and family values.

One example of this is a client who always includes an agenda item in their annual meeting where the grandparents make a presentation to the whole family about some aspect of their early lives. Pictures and videos usually accompany the stories. The grandchildren are on the edge of their seats, learning about their grandma and grandpa's lives. Today's technology makes it relatively easy to capture these wonderful stories that highlight family values and life experiences. The presentations are videotaped and a disc is made for each family member. This is a priceless gift to the future.

Another example is to create an ethical will. This old Jewish tradition has senior-generation family members share the critical values they want to pass on. Topics for an ethical will can include:

- Success as I see it
- Mistakes I learned from
- My happiest hours
- Why I love you
- What spirituality means to me
- Stories with deep personal meaning
- People or events that have shaped my life
- Familial obligation
- Favorite scripture passages
- Actions for which I would like to ask forgiveness

Select any or all from the list to share at future family meetings. Families enjoy wonderful, positive feelings when parents share their stories; stories nurture bonding and often produce a few tears and smiles when people come so closely together.

I know of truly ambitious individuals who have written their life stories. You can record your story in book form or create a video to share with the entire family. Many resources are available to help you capture these family memories. Over the years, I have created two videos about my life and have shared them with my family. The first one is about my work; the second is about my values and stories from my past.

One of my greatest thrills in giving to the future was introducing my grandchildren to the arts. We frequently attend the Children's Theater and Minnesota Orchestra.

Another part of my legacy is helping to provide for a good education. I enroll each of my grandchildren in a book club on their first Christmas. Learning has always been a big part of my life, and I want to make sure my grandkids learn to enjoy reading.

These examples emphasize the nonfinancial aspects of inheritance that, according to the Allianz study, are the most important. As you fine-tune your legacy, take time to engage your family. Share some of the stories and meaningful events of your life. Share with them the events and people who have shaped your life. This could be your greatest—and most appreciated—gift to the future success of your family.

My Parents' Legacy

When talking about investments, one often hears, "Past performance is no guarantee of future results." One also hears that "our children are our investment in the future." Who can imagine a parent who has no dreams for his or her child's success? Even before the moment they see their newborn baby—through the nursery glass or at the instant of birth—most parents have already begun to imagine the success of their child and formulate hopes for them.

For parents in a family-owned business, these hopes double-down because there is a business involved. Future possibilities are clearly in place. This is where a parent must be able to discern the difference between their own dreams and their children's dreams. Parents must be careful not to project their own dreams onto their children and be careful not to "live" through them.

For a new generation growing up in the family business, this implies a dichotomy. A parent may or may not want their child to become part of the family business. Yet the growing child's wishes could be different from what the parent wants. So how can a parent's past performance—or legacy—produce future results?

In my experience, successful mothers and fathers invest in their children by helping them build their own dreams. Parents help their children discover their gifts, their passions in life, and the confidence to act on their own. Regardless of a parent's desire for his or her children to eventually work in the family business, a parent's selfless priority is to help each child follow his or her own intentions.

Like most parents, I was determined to give my children more opportunities than I had growing up. My own father was a sweet, kind, and gentle person. He worked on the railroad and at the barbershop. We were, as they say, of modest means.

My fondest memories of my dad are connected to his values and the things we did together. For example, he cut my hair when I was a small boy. Simple as this was, these haircuts became moments when I felt special and loved. They are part of his legacy to me. I certainly did not realize at the time that they were his investment in me or that they would produce something in me.

I memorialized the barbershop experience in a poem.

Special moments with Dad
All those stories about white hair and being called Cotton
The special moments in the barber chair—with green Jerri's Tonic
The Hotel Claude barbershop with all its stories of past heroes
The follow-up breakfasts at the bus, which I now know as
    Mickey's Diner
The one-block walk to Applebaum's to get the week's groceries
Hearing about the years on the Rock Island Railroad and the
    four generations of our family that worked there
Having you hold me in your arms and singing Beautiful Dreamer
Feeling the pride of knowing that I was your son
—Tom Hubler, 1999

My father periodically took me along to the switchyards when he worked for the railroad, and I got to ride in the engine and the caboose. Imagine how thrilling for a small boy! During those times, my father introduced me to the car men, who were workers employed in the lowest jobs at the yard; they also happened to be people of color. The way my father introduced me to the car men made me feel like I was meeting the president of the railroad. He treated them with dignity and respect. His actions taught me to do the same. That was his legacy, now instilled in me.

The same is true of my mother, Lou—she has a lasting legacy of what she had hoped for me. Lou was more outgoing and extroverted than my dad and had a positive influence on me in terms of learning about racial issues. As a licensed practical nurse at a local hospital, Lou would often invite black female co-workers to our home for socializing and cocktails. It was something that normally was not practiced in our mostly white neighborhood.

Another lasting influence of Lou's was her love of music. She loved taking my sister, Judy, and me to pops concerts that featured both light classical music and a figure skating review. Later, she encouraged me to take up the clarinet when I was in the fifth grade, and I played in the band from junior high school through my freshman college year. As a result of Lou sharing her passion for music with me, I became familiar with classical music, and my life has been changed and richly rewarded by learning about classical composers and listening to their music.

But, more important than anything else, my mother's legacy was her courage. She suffered from the illness of alcoholism most of her life and probably had undiagnosed PTSD from early trauma in her life. Lou's gift to me was her courage to address these issues and receive treatment when she was sixty-two years old. For the last ten years of her life, she was sober and invited to work on the drug unit of the hospital where she worked. She also was an invited speaker for the treatment unit, where she courageously shared her story in the hopes that others, too, could divert their energy and positively turn their lives around.

These memories of my parents accumulated as small gifts—mere moments in passing—that became an extraordinary influence on how I approached people of color in my own life. I'm sure they helped lead me to my decision to adopt two African American infants.

And this marks a key point regarding legacy: What you do becomes what you are and embeds an attitude in your child. Legacy seeds are planted in demonstrations.

Family Legacy in Action

One of my favorite family business clients, George, did a terrific job of creating a legacy for his adult children and grandchildren. Every summer he held family meetings at his hobby farm. George and his wife, Nan, hosted their adult children and all their grandchildren. They orchestrated educational, business-related, and fun experiences at these gatherings. The adults would convene to discuss issues affecting their family business and the impact of wealth on themselves and their children (the business was quite successful). They brainstormed about how not to let wealth corrupt their family.

The family went beyond merely brainstorming about the impact of wealth. At these summer meetings, they included the grandchildren in brief, educational discussions about money and family values. Discussions like this were especially important because it helped the grandchildren internalize their family's values about money. The legacy included these ideas.

One year, George and Nan combined the summer meeting with a trip to the family's business, which was thirty miles from the hobby farm. The family took a tour of the facilities and enjoyed lunch in the boardroom. George shared a presentation about the million-dollar company he had started in his garage.

In this and many other ways, George played a major part in organizing and leading the annual summer family meetings. George and Nan were full partners in the process, but George's energy and enthusiasm prompted his adult children and grandchildren to want to participate. By being involved himself, George demonstrated what was important. And those demonstrations became the roots of his legacy.

Legacy Through the Generations

As many successful family-business clients have demonstrated, parents involved in a family business will spend thirty to forty years representing their legacies. I say representing because it is most often unconscious or subconscious. A parent's legacy arises from how he or she did what they did—*how* they lived their lives. Viewed across time, creating a legacy seems like a daunting task. It can produce both positive and negative responses. But a legacy accumulates over the years through the pattern of an individual's life. And by living a life of respect, intention, joy, and forgiveness, those values are passed on to be mirrored by the children.

One of my favorite reflections on legacy comes from the 1957 film *The Bridge on the River Kwai*. It's World War II, and British prisoners of war are forced by their Japanese captors to build a bridge in the Burmese jungle. When the bridge is completed, the British commander reflects on his life and long military career:

> *I've been thinking. Tomorrow it will be [twenty-eight] years to the day that I've been in the service. Twenty-eight years in peace and war. I don't suppose I've been at home more than ten months in all that time. Still, it's been a good life. I loved India. I wouldn't have had it any other way. But there are times when suddenly you realize you're nearer the end than the beginning. And you wonder, you ask yourself, what the sum total of your life represents. What difference your being there at any time made to anything. Hardly made any difference at all, really, particularly in comparison with*

other men's careers. I don't know whether that kind of thinking's very healthy; but I must admit I've had some thoughts on those lines from time to time.

As I've noted previously, when parents reach their sixties and seventies, they start to ponder whether their life has made a difference. It is not just a challenging question, but possibly a gut-wrenching one. In those moments, parents wonder if their families have appreciated their hard work and dedication. Every human being wants to feel valued and appreciated, but I think this need is particularly strong among families who have a business.

And that marks a second key point regarding legacy. A parent's legacy is verified by the appreciation of his or her children. Without verbal appreciation, a parent may question his or her value to the family.

FROM THE CASE STUDY FILES: BILL AND MATT

My clients, father Bill and his son Matt, were caught up in a misunderstanding. Bill was a successful seventy-year-old businessman. He was active in his community as a philanthropist and strongly desired to continue his contributions. Bill wanted Matt to recognize him for what he had accomplished. Matt felt it was unnecessary and awkward. Yet I know that even though Matt was reluctant to validate his father, he wanted the very same thing from Bill. Each was playing an emotional game of chicken, waiting for the other to make the first move. Waiting for the other to blink may sound childish, but I find it often in my practice. It is a behavior that can be deeply ingrained.

I helped Bill and Matt gain the courage to ask each other for what they wanted. For that to happen, they first needed to forgive one another. Then they could start fresh in their father-son relationship—no small task when the father was seventy and the son was forty-five. Attitudes may be cemented, a point of false pride; a standoff becomes more important than a resolution. I have found that the members of the younger generation must usually take the initiative and reach out to their parents.

As I get older, I also realize that I'm nearer to the end than the beginning of my life. My priorities have changed, and I'm much more aware of the legacy I will leave to my adult children and grandchildren. Actively engaging children and grandchildren in our family's key values of giving and education has been part of that legacy. Yet truly, it is the demonstrations of your life, accumulated over time, that become the legacy by which your children and grandchildren remember you.

The senior generation must be willing to ask their adult children for the validation they need and deserve. At the same time, they should share their stories, experiences, and values with their families. This sharing is the investment in the next generation. It becomes your legacy, which likely pays dividends for generations to come.

7

ADVICE FOR ADVISORS

Family Business Consultants as Leaders

Working with family businesses as a consultant is one of the most awesome responsibilities I can imagine. It incorporates managing family issues and concerns, as well as business issues and concerns, and the interrelationship between the two. The impact of choices made by the consultant can have far-reaching effects for both family and business that can impact generations of family members.

As the field of family business consulting evolves, and there are more and more practitioners and other professionals such as lawyers, accountants, and insurance professionals working with family businesses, there will also concurrently be more discussions about "client failures." From the consultant's perspective, these are situations where, in retrospect, the choices made in regard to assisting the client did not achieve the desired result—in terms of either the family or the business issues.

In my own practice of family business consulting, there are times that I look back and realize that an intervention or a suggestion to a client was inappropriate. What has enabled me to evolve and be more effective is the opportunity to meet with my study group to analyze and understand what went wrong and what I could have done differently.

Fritz Perls (1893–1970) was often quoted as saying that we only learn from our mistakes. Len Hirsch, one of my mentors, often said that clients never make mistakes; it's always the responsibility of the consultant. For me, being willing to talk about these mistakes or failures more publicly or to present a program on the topic of client failures would take even greater courage, in addition to candor and humility. To do so, a presenter would need to expose his or her professional work, consulting mistakes, and something about him or herself in analyzing a case failure publicly.

I have a tremendous amount of admiration for some presenters who were willing to do just that at a recent Family Firm Institute conference. Their courage and willingness to take on this daunting task and expose themselves, their philosophies, and choices to all who attended demonstrated the kind of leadership I think is important for the continued evolution of the field of family business consulting. It will take leadership on the part of all practitioners who are willing to publicly examine their work and take on the responsibilities that are part of working with families and business.

In his chapter "Leading from Within: Out of the Shadow, into the Light," Parker Palmer[i] quotes Vaclav Havel on the notion of leadership as it applies across the board beyond politicians and heads of nation states to classroom teachers and so on. His point is that anyone in a position of power is a leader in the broad sense of the word and, therefore, has a duty to take on the responsibilities that go with that type of leadership. I believe that this is clearly the case in the context of family-owned businesses. As long as we continue to work with family businesses, each of us has a special responsibility to explore what is going on inside our own conscience. Otherwise, we have the potential to do more harm than good.

In his book *The Heart Aroused: Poetry and the Preservation of the Soul in Corporate America*, David Whyte discusses this same issue from a little different perspective in his second chapter entitled, "Beowulf."[ii] Beowulf is a masculine story about the descent into the waters of the unconscious. All of us stand at the edge of our own inner pool of darkness and its monsters, which, out of fear, we have a tendency to want to avoid.

Whyte addresses the modern corporation and the equivalent of those repressed monsters from Beowulf that lie just below the surface of our professional lives. He lists a few of the many. The most important include:

> *Unresolved parent-child relationships that play out into rigid company hierarchies, paternal management systems and dependent employees; unresolved emotional demands individuals may have of fellow workers, but many never admit to themselves; the refusal to come to terms with an abused childhood, the subsequent longing for self-protection and the wielding of organizational power and control at any cost to gain that protection. Perhaps the parent of all of these vulnerabilities is Beowulf's mother herself, the deep physical shame that we are not enough, will never be enough, and can never measure up.*

While Whyte talks about these in the context of the corporate world, they are certainly present for all consultants. If we think about Vaclav Havel's admonition to take responsibility for our own consciousness lest our involvement create more harm than good, we are then compelled to confront the depths of our souls and move to a deeper understanding of our inner experiences. Each of us has a family of origin that constantly influences our perspective, our intervention, and our advice to clients. The more we understand these influences, the more effective we can be in not projecting our own experiences onto our clients. Palmer comments:

> *Great leadership comes from people who have made the downward journey through violence and terror, who have touched the deep place where we are in community with each other, and who can help take the rest of us to that place. That is what great leadership is all about.*

All family business consultants and other professionals who work with family businesses have a responsibility to go inside themselves and develop a more effective understanding of their own inner experiences. We must begin to ponder, in a deeper and more systematic way, our personal and professional experiences that could negatively affect the work we do with our family business clients.

To create light out of shadow, Palmer calls us to address five areas of shadow that could affect and be projected onto our work with family business clients. Since most of our world as consultants is extroverted, it is often difficult to recognize our projections, as well as take a more introspective approach to our work and to the bias we bring to our work.

I will first cite Palmer's five areas of shadow and then go back and discuss how they might apply to our work with family-owned businesses. The first is "a deep insecurity about our own identity and self-worth." The second shadow has to do with the perception that "the universe is essentially hostile to human interests and that life is fundamentally a battleground." The third shadow in leaders and consultants is what he calls "'functional atheism'—the belief that the ultimate responsibility for everything rests with me." The fourth shadow is fear around the natural chaos of life, and the final shadow is the denial of death. Each of these shadows has a potential negative impact on our consulting of family-owned businesses and warrants further examination.

First, because consultants are in an externally focused profession, it is very difficult to recognize the fact that, underneath all of their self-assuredness, they have issues and concerns like everyone else about their own sense of identity and self-worth. It is sometimes manifested in their work with clients and, if the consultant-leader is unaware of it, he or she can project fears and insecurity onto their clients and end up creating systems and solutions that deprive others of dealing with their own issues and identity.

In his work in building learning organizations, Peter Senge[iii] often talks about people becoming their roles. This happens to consultants who are unavailable to deal with their own inner fears about their identity. In addition, they are often afraid to challenge their clients in unexplored areas of their own identity. Instead, the consultant takes on the role of expert and often robs the client of opportunities for growth and development of his or her own potential.

The gift according to Palmer is that if I am able to ponder this question, I will know that who I am does not depend on what I do. Knowing this about ourselves frees us as consultants to be flexible and create options that will benefit our clients.

The second shadow has to do with seeing the world as hostile to human interest and life as a battleground. I have often heard lawyers say, "It is necessary to eat what you kill." The battleground analogy often becomes a self-fulfilling prophecy. Essentially, this mentality is born out of a sense of scarcity rather than abundance. As a result, professionals don't refer when they should, and they take on the philosophy of Ralph's Pretty Good Grocery in Lake Woebegon, Minnesota. Ralph's philosophy is, "If we don't have it here, you don't need it." As a result, consultants fail to collaborate with each other, and they begin to operate under what I describe as "delusions of adequacy." They don't learn from each other or benefit from the synergy of their different perspectives on how to assist their clients. The gift for those consultant leaders who are willing to take the challenge is the knowledge that the universe is working together for good and a tremendous sense of abundance. Collaborating with other professionals will not diminish their practice, and they will not lose influence with their clients.

The third shadow is "functional atheism." Consultants who operate with the belief that ultimate responsibility for everything rests with them and that they make it happen are basically disempowering their clients. Their assumption is, "Just let me do it." They are often plagued with workaholism and burnout. The gift, again if they are willing to ponder this shadow, is the realization that they are not the only act in town. They are co-creators with their clients and other professionals. Again, it is the synergy of the work with the consulting team that creates the best solutions. Ultimately, the challenge is to trust others—not only other professionals but also the clients themselves, for it is generally their insights and their ideas that create the best solutions.

The fourth shadow is fear around the natural chaos of life. Fear is something that affects consultants as they work with the daunting challenges of being involved in a family-owned business. As a result of forgetting that creativity comes out of chaos, some consultants are prone to create structures, solutions, and a sense of rigidity that sometimes is not in the best service of their clients. It represents to some extent a failure to integrate the J and the P on the Myers-Briggs Type Indicator. The judging and perceptive function is the fourth of the four polarities discussed in the Myers-Briggs Type Indicator.[iv] The judging function is organized and structured, while the perceptive function is more spontaneous and goes with the flow. Structure and premature closure often are not in the best interest of the client. Essentially, the consultants are avoiding the issues of change they were brought in to deal with and avoiding doing it differently. Often, as a result, they create outmoded technologies and simple solutions that are inappropriate. H. L. Mencken (1880–1956) once commented on this issue when he said, "For every complex problem there are a multitude of simple solutions—all of which are wrong."

The gift of encountering this shadow and going inward is the realization that creation comes out of chaos. However, it requires the discipline of learning to live in the moment—something that is difficult not only for our clients but also for ourselves. We come to realize that change can only occur in the moment, and it is essential that we learn the discipline of that challenge. It also requires us to accept the notion that people and organizations, despite our intuition to the contrary, thrive on chaos. If they can stay with it long enough and be disciplined not to create premature solutions, they will have positive results they could never have imagined.

The final shadow is the shadow of death. All the work that consultants of family-owned businesses do in regard to the ownership-succession process, as well as leadership succession, implicitly has to do with the issue of loss and death. Unless the consultant has come to terms with that issue in his or her own life, it is going to be problematic for the clients.

As a result of not integrating and coming to terms with that issue, consultants will artificially maintain the status quo and avoid helping the client deal with the letting-go and change issues in the family business succession transition. Often, a consultant is concerned about a negative evaluation, a public failure, or getting a "pink slip," so he or she avoids dealing with the critical transition issues in a succession planning process. Or, he or she may continue to try to work with and/or change a client beyond that which is reasonable.

The ability to ponder these mysteries and the shadow of death allows us to realize that death is natural. This is the gift. When we can allow things to die, new systems and new life will emerge. Ultimately, we come to the realization that death is an old friend. Denise Levertov's poem "Talking to Grief" (1975) captures the essence, for me, of the integration of this issue. It has to do with recognizing that winter is coming and that I need to let that dog live under my porch so I can come to terms with the issues of change and loss in my own life. In doing so, I can avoid projecting those issues onto my clients.

> *Talking to Grief*
> Ah, Grief, I should not treat you
> like a homeless dog
> who comes to the back door
> for a crust, for a meatless bone.
> I should trust you.
>
> I should coax you
> into the house and give you
> your own corner,
> a worn mat to lie on,
> your own water dish.

You think I don't know you've been living
under my porch.
You long for your real place to be readied
before winter comes. You need
your name,
your collar and tag. You need
the right to warn off intruders,
to consider
my house your own
and me your person
and yourself
my own dog.

In my own practice, I encounter these shadows regularly. In some instances, I am pleased with the results. In other instances, I am disappointed with my response.

A client situation I encountered illustrates the first of two shadows that often challenge me as a consultant. "Functional atheism" is a frequent shadow of mine and manifests itself in my doing too much and not trusting the client. It combines with the first shadow, insecurity, to create a situation in which I, as a consultant, begin to operate with delusions of adequacy and think I know what is best for the client.

In this specific situation, a second-generation owner-entrepreneur in his early seventies and his spouse were at a family-business planning meeting with their three adult children and their spouses. The purpose was to initiate succession-planning discussions. I was anticipating that some stressful family revelations would come out during the meeting, so prior to the meeting, I had asked the owner-entrepreneur to be prepared and available, in an emotional sense, to his oldest son who was active in the business along with his sister and her husband. Quite to my surprise, the father came to the meeting with a letter he wanted to distribute at the outset.

I made it quite clear to the entrepreneur that I had a very specific process planned for the meeting. I told him it would be inappropriate to distribute copies of the letter to the family at this point in time because it would upset my sequence and schedule of events.

After his second and third request to share the letter, it finally dawned on me how inappropriate I was in not letting him do so. This was my delusion of adequacy and thinking that I knew better than the client. As I finally realized this, I then suggested to the client that he read the letter to his family and distribute copies later.

This turned out to be one of the most profound meetings I have ever experienced. Rather haltingly and with tears, the client began to read his letter and share a metaphor about his life. He talked about his blessings, and how he and his wife had been on a journey up the mountain for the past fifty years. "The summit," he said, "was foremost a truly great family relationship supported by a thriving business free and clear of debt. Obviously we have fallen short of our summit."

He went on to say that the time had come for him and his wife to descend the mountain and allow their children to take responsibility for their own journey. By this time, there was not a dry eye in the room. The father's story pierced the cold, emotional facade. It not only changed the course of the meeting, but it also made it possible for the family to reconnect emotionally and spend the first Easter in ten years together as a family.

I am humbled to think how close I came to overlooking this significant opportunity for the family. I learned a lesson I will never forget.

The second shadow I meet regularly relates to loss and death. This shadow is the most profound in that it requires that I, as a result of client situations, regularly confront the loss issues in my own life.

I mentioned earlier how hard it is to explore issues with clients if those areas are unexplored in the consultant's own life. This is particularly true in the shadow area of loss and death. A friend once told me that I am the most optimistic person he knows. He said that I am the only one he knows who would try to get a thirty-three-inch refrigerator through a thirty-one-inch door. I am sure that a major part of that optimism in client situations is driven by my avoidance of loss issues, related to the loss of two sons at birth and the sometimes-worries about losing my third. I realize that, in this area, I am clearly vulnerable to creating unrealistic expectations, and sometimes a false sense of optimism, for clients. On the other hand, I realize the benefit of having explored the blessings of loss in that it enables me to help clients explore an area of family business loss that might otherwise go unaddressed and adversely effect the succession planning process.

The closing line in Mary Oliver's poem "When Death Comes" (1992) is an inspiration to me as I encounter these loss issues. She writes:

> When it's over I want to say: all my life
> I was a bride married to amazement.
> I was a bridegroom, taking the world into my arms.
> When it's over, I don't want to wonder if I have made of my life
>   something particular, and real.
> I don't want to find myself sighing and frightened, or full of
>   argument.
> I don't want to end up simply having visited the world.

When it comes to consulting with family businesses, I clearly do not want to have only visited this world. I want to make something of my life experiences and my shadows that also allows me to bring light to my clients.

As the field of family business continues to evolve, it will be important to continue to encourage workshops and study groups that support the idea of learning from our mistakes. At the same time, it is equally important and equally courageous to continue to support the idea and value of our inner work of dealing with our shadows. We need to acknowledge and admit our mistakes, and use them as opportunities to bring us to higher levels of sophistication with our family business clients. The interdisciplinary study group that I participate in has been an excellent resource for me to understand my biases and how I can be more effective and bring light to my family business clients. Each of us has the responsibility to accept the leadership challenge of Vaclav Havel and continue to the best of our ability to bring light rather than darkness to the clients we encounter.

Are You Trained to Ride the Elephant in the Room?

Picture this: You are an accountant, a lawyer, a financial planner, or a technical professional. You are in a client's office, discussing an issue. You understand the facts. You are probing for specifics, and suddenly the owner-entrepreneur gets up, closes the office door, sits back down, and looks at you with tears in his or her eyes. Are you the therapist?

How about this: You're part of a meeting with the members of a family business. Something is said (maybe you said something innocently), and suddenly voices rise and accusations snap back and forth among family members. Are you the arbitrator?

I had an accountant friend once tell me that whenever a client shut the door, his palms started to sweat. He knew the client wanted to share something emotional. When it happened, my friend felt unsure of what to say in this scenario and felt uncomfortable about what to do.

Of course it was uncomfortable—he wasn't trained for it!

Few technical professionals are trained to deal with emotional issues, humans in stress, or boiling altercations. They are the experts who analyze the facts, make rational judgments, and offer logical solutions. Handling client emotions is not taught in business school.

But there's another side to the coin. Despite the fact that you weren't trained to deal with emotions, you have your own family experience to draw from to help you respond to your client's family situation. As a result, and without making your personal response dominant, you can share your own experiences and emotionally connect with your clients to assist them in managing their emotional issues. The most significant skill you have is your capacity to connect, listen, and bear witness to your client's emotional experience. Although you are not a trained professional, your capacity to emotionally connect is critical.

When it is appropriate, I encourage you to partner with a trained professional—such as a psychologically trained family business consultant or a psychologist, social worker, or marriage and family therapist—to provide the necessary support for your client. This is an example of the multidisciplinary approach necessary to successfully work with family businesses. No one professional has all the answers.

Countertransference

In the behavioral sciences, an unconscious response based on your own experience is called "countertransference." It means that without knowing it, we project our experience onto our clients. Or in the opposite way, clients project their issues onto the technical professional, becoming angry at them for unresolved emotional issues from their past. This subconscious transference can create problems—for you and for your client—particularly if you react. But then how should you act? You weren't taught how to do it!

Family business consultants, particularly those with a psychological background, are trained to manage issues of countertransference. Emotional issues can occur with any client, and they can occur even when the family business consultant is a behavioral professional. But they also have the preparation and experience to resolve emotional issues in a way that adds value for the client.

You are probably already aware of the clues to when it would be helpful to have a family business consultant support your efforts. See whether you have run into these common situations.

Clues that you've been asked to ride the elephant

A major issue for many families and their businesses is a lack of communication. This is a red flag that could mean it is time to bring in a family business consultant who is trained in the area of family communication. When poor communication skills go unchecked, family members find it hard to collaborate and work as a team. Individuals are often poor at expressing their feelings and wants, and they are poor at listening. A trained professional can help individuals learn good communication skills.

Another moment for a competent behavioral professional comes during succession planning—a time you would think is merely a technical, factual effort. And that's true, in part. You help the business resolve complex financial, tax, business planning, and ownership and leadership issues. However, there are often—I would even say usually—complicated family issues hiding in every succession plan. Having a trained psychologically minded family business consultant adds value to smooth and guide a succession plan's implementation. Here's an example: Business differences were eroding the positive relationship between a father and his son. They were at odds over taking financial risks and growing the business. Dad saw it one way; the son saw it another. But what they felt was a father-son difference I saw as a business planning issue. I engaged the father and the son in a strategic business planning process. In the end, they mutually developed a completely different strategy to grow the business that alleviated the father's concerns about financial risk and that fed the son's excitement about leading a growing business. Everybody won!

Engaging with a family business consultant

You recognize the clues, but how do you talk about bringing in a family business consultant?

Technical professionals generally help clients through the planning process in one of four areas I refer to as the Four Essential Plans: (1) a business plan, (2) an ownership plan, (3) a management and leadership plan or (4) a family plan.

But from my perspective, the best place to start is in the center of the model—the core purpose. Understanding a client's core purpose gives you many insights about how to approach an entre- preneur who has concerns. The second ring (in darker grey) represents what moti- vates owner-entrepreneurs to do succession planning. Certainly, economic security

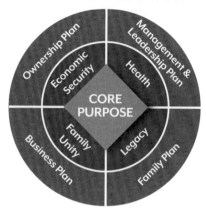

and health are important motivators, but equally if not more impor- tantly are concerns about family unity and legacy.

Family unity is important because parents don't want to be in their sixties or seventies and have their family and business torn apart by business and financial differences.

Similarly, a person's legacy is a powerful motivator. At some emo- tional level, all entrepreneurs understand they are "playing the back nine." They realize that in order to continue their impact in the world, they need to pass along their values, life learnings, and other insights so that what is important to them lives on in their descendants.

Another aspect of legacy pertains to how someone feels they will be remembered. As people get older, they begin to wonder about whether their lives have meant something and whether their life has made a difference to anyone. This validation seeking is a huge moti- vator for entrepreneurs.

That's why I developed the Inside-Out Succession Plan™ model (see Chapter 5 for more on this). It recognizes these motivations and uses them to calmly ask entrepreneurs critical and often emotional ques- tions about their core purpose, the importance of their family's uni- ty, and what they desire as a legacy.

I engage the entrepreneur and spouse in discussions framed by their core purpose, family unity, and legacy. I include the spouse because he or she is usually extremely influential. The spouse is often the one who seeks outside help to solve family business issues and can draw together all parties—entrepreneur, family members, technical professional, and family-business consultant. This person can be your willing champion for bringing up emotional issues that resolve business expectations.

Rather than telling the entrepreneur what to do, you can have greater influence at lower risk by asking open-ended questions. Here are a few:

- What are your goals?

- How do you want to be remembered?

- What would happen if . . . ?

- Is there any possibility . . . ?

- How are you feeling about . . . ?

- What do you want?

- What are you willing to do to make that happen?

- How could you provide leadership to your family to discuss the possibility of doing . . . ?

- What would happen if family members could forgive one another for what has happened?

- What are the pros and cons of using an outside resource to help the family discuss this matter?

These are just a sampling of the questions I regularly use. Use your own intuition to ask questions that help your client deal with the tough, emotional stuff.

(For ways to help your clients cope with difficult situations, see "Twenty-three Ways to Deal with the Tough Stuff in Family Business™" on page 199 of the Appendix.)

Afterword
What's my *legacy?*

When I reviewed the first draft of my book, it was like my professional life flashing across my eyes. It was like remembering and seeing
all of the things I had been taught throughout my career come to
life in the stories of the families I have worked with throughout my
career. The collective experience of seeing and reliving these stories made me realize how unique my perspective is and how blessed I am by the families who have shared their lives with me.

There are several themes that have contributed to the development
of my perspective that weave their way into the book. The first and
most obvious one is the impact of my family and the role my parents played in shaping who I am. I know everyone's family of origin is very impactful, but in my case, my experiences caused me to
develop the important ability to connect emotionally. As a result,
emotional intelligence is one of the lenses through which I view the
world and is outlined in this book.

Years ago, as I made the transition from being a family therapist to
consultant, I applied for and received a Bush Leadership Fellow-
ship, an award granted to mid-career professionals to study new
areas of interest. My thesis was that mental health professionals do
not do within their own systems what they teach their clients to do,
and my goal was to help the nonprofits get their acts together. It
was a brilliant idea (if I do say so myself), and I received the dollars
I needed to be able to go to school. But it never dawned on me that
there was no money in a nonprofit's budget to pay for those kinds
of services.

Then I began to do work for law firms and physician groups that
were having a terrible time managing their differences. One of the
partners, Steve Swartz, who was on the hiring committee of one of

the first law firms I worked with, asked if we could work together to consult with professional organizations. We were moving in that direction until, in 1981, I was in Cleveland to deliver a paper at a conference with Ernesto Poza. After our presentation was over, I came across an unpublished paper by Dick Beckhart and Elaine Kepner on family-owned businesses. I read the paper on the airplane back to the Twin Cities and told Steve that this was a much better blend of our backgrounds. We then began to do work with family-owned businesses at a time when only a handful of people in the country were doing so—and none in the Twin Cities. Back then, there was only one university program at Wharton at the University of Pennsylvania, whereas today there are more than one hundred family business programs at universities in the United States. Our firm, Hubler/Swartz, became nationally known as a family therapist and a lawyer working together—the first multi-disciplinary team working in the United States with family businesses—and was later sold to the accounting firm McGladrey Pullen. Those early years of Hubler/Swartz were a tremendous learning experience about family businesses, and I've always been grateful to Steve for his insights and partnership.

I'm sure the reason I committed so much time, money, and energy to post-graduate education was to deepen my understanding of Family Systems Theory. The Family Therapy Institute with Merle Fosum and Rene Schwartz played a big part in my formation and the development of my perspective about families. It is also the reason I participated in two post-graduate training programs at the Gestalt Institute of Cleveland with Len Hirsch as my mentor.

My understanding about people, emotions, and how to create change were formulated in those years. The importance of focusing on the positive and the answer were a part of the evolution of my philosophy.

Related to this is the importance of mindfulness and being in the moment, and the work of Jon Kabat-Zinn has also had significant influence on how I view the world. More recently, Amit Sood of the

Mayo Clinic has further developed my thinking regarding mindfulness and stress reduction.

Another obvious conclusion is the initial influence of my Catholic upbringing, which influenced the development of my spirituality and my soul. While I did not have much formal Catholic education as a young child, the impact of the priests and sisters were a significant example to me of the importance of spirit and serving others. This spiritual development was further enhanced by my understanding of spirituality through the work of Gail Straub, David Gershon, and their Empowerment Workshop. In addition, the independent study I did at the Hudson Institute in Santa Barbara on spirituality further guided my work on development of soul and the creation of my philosophy on Life Career Planning™.

Another theme that runs through the book is legacy. Laura Nash defines legacy as your gift to the future to help others find success. I always add that another aspect of legacy is how people are going to be remembered.

What I hope readers understand, and what I hope to be remembered for, is the importance of soul, living a purposeful life, and spirituality. To me, these three are inextricably combined. The essence of soul, for me on an individual basis, is discovering and living your purpose for the benefit of your family, your community, and your higher power. For a family business, it is continuing your sense of purpose with your combined sense of values and manifesting them.

One of the most unusual ways living a purposeful and spiritual life has manifested itself in my life has been through beekeeping. For forty years, beekeeping was an integral part of my life. The connection between beekeeping, living a purposeful life, and spirituality comes in the pollination process. Pollination is a $16 billion industry in this country and is the source of increasing the yield on all the things we eat that come from the earth, i.e., vegetables, fruits, and nuts. Pollination is also a metaphor for everything I do with my family business clients. I use my spiritual gifts to assist the family in developing or realizing their gifts. The realization of their gifts and the solution of their challenges is like the honey I receive from the bees—so smooth, sweet, and satisfying.

The essence of my spiritual purpose is contained within an aphorism I created and recite to myself every morning:

> *Spirituality is an adventure and is the essence of my life.*
> *It allows me to celebrate (share) my passion, my joy, and*
> *my love.*
> *It connects me to my soul and creates my communion with*
> *you and with the universe.*

As a result, happiness in life—in this case, my life—is the utilization of my gifts for the benefit of my family, my community, my clients, and my higher power.

Related to all of this is the importance of effective communication where understanding occurs through effective listening. Listening is the communication skill we use the most, but for which we get the least amount of training.

Another theme is the importance of love. For me, M. Scott Peck in *The Road Less Traveled* defines love the best when he says love is the promotion of the spiritual wellbeing of another. I try to promote the concept in the O part of the B.O.S.S. and the various synonyms used that include kything and psychic energy.

One aspect of the work I do with family businesses is to learn how to speak your truth with kindness, care, and respect—Amit Sood's lenses with which he proposes we interpret our world of experiences. Those lenses of compassion, acceptance, forgiveness, and gratitude summarize the themes of the book that I hope have become the core of my life and my work.

Compassion is daily kindness to others. We often underestimate the power of a smile, a kind word, or a moment taken to listen to another human being.

Acceptance is the realization that I don't control the world or, in particular, the people or circumstances of my life. For me, AA and Al-Anon say it best in the first two of the twelve Steps: We admit in Step One that we are powerless and our lives have become unmanageable, and Step Two goes on to say only a power greater than ourselves can restore us to sanity. The insanity that occurs in family businesses exists when we try to change other people. It just doesn't work—we can only change ourselves.

Forgiveness is the core of any successful family. The benefits associated with forgiveness are great. When forgiveness occurs, it allows you to receive more love from the important people in your life (family and close friends), and it re-energizes relationships.

Gratitude is the recognition of the blessings of our lives. Robert Emmons said, "Gratitude is the way the heart remembers kindness—cherished interaction with others, compassionate actions of strangers, surprise gifts and everyday blessings."

As I reflect on my career and life, I want to express my gratitude to all of those who have reached out to me and seen things in me that I could hardly imagine were there. To the many clients who shared their lives with me, I want to express my deepest gratitude and thanks for your trust in me and for allowing me to share your journey.

—*TH*

Acknowledgements

I want to express my gratitude to the editors of my written work who have supported me over the years:

The first is Joe Astrachan, one of the first editors of *Family Business Review*. His thoughtful, patient, and kind encouragement to a new writer enabled me to publish some of my first articles in *FBR*.

Another source of editorial support came from Leo Rickertsen, whose insights over frequent and loving breakfasts challenged my thinking about family businesses and, more importantly, life.

Mary Lilja, the editor of this book, has been a tremendous inspiration through her own family business experiences. Mary has pestered, cajoled, and pleaded with me for the past fifteen years to write this book. She has been a continual source of irritation and love, for which I am grateful.

Another major influence on the development of my perspective on family businesses came from the multidisciplinary study group that I participated in for twenty-five years. The initial participants who challenged my thinking were Gerald LeVan, John Messervey, Jeff Rothstein, Glenn Swogger, and Tom Zanecchia.

Appendix

Tom's Favorite Terms

Throughout my career, I've often used specific terms, phrases, and techniques that are applicable to a wide range of family business situations. Some phrases are my own, and others I've adapted from other professionals.

I talked about these terms extensively throughout the book, and there are times when employing them can be useful for business planning, connecting with family, and diffusing tense situations.

Here is a quick recap of the terms used in this book:

B.O.S.S.
Family businesses must balance the needs of the business with the needs of the family. The B.O.S.S. acronym was developed by Sherod Miller[i] with the goal to create win-win solutions that honor the Common Family Vision™ and help promote a common family point of view.

B stands for — What does the Business need in order to be successful?

O stands for — What do you want for your Other family members involved in the business regarding what they want? Reciprocal commitment to each other's success—for example, if two siblings are working together, they need to each know that the other sibling is committed to helping them get what they want.

S stands for — What do you want for your Self? But a company can't survive based on only self-interest. It must be in the context of the greater family vision.

S stands for — What do you want for the other Stakeholders? This includes the family as a whole, the employees, the customers, the vendors, and the board. The goal is create win-win solutions that honor the family while also satisfying the other stakeholders.

Family Forgiveness Ritual™
This is a method of taking a family's religious tradition and creating a ceremony that draws on the family's fundamental values of love, generosity, and sense of abundance to bring about forgiveness. I use this ritual with families in the context of an overall family business consultation. The ritual is a helpful tool to avert escalating tensions, continued strain on relationships, and even legal actions.

Hubler's Speck of Dust Theory™
To avoid conflict and preserve family relationships, many families avoid talking about their differences. They keep sweeping them under the rug because it might upset family gatherings, events, or holidays. Yet by not discussing differences, those little specks of dust collect into a big pile as problems fester away.

Kything
This Scottish word means "connecting at a spiritual level." It is not psychological; it is a spiritual presentation of your soul to another. I encourage family members to think about one another daily through brief kything. Kything represents the vision statements of family members that are put in the third person and reflect what that person wants, needs, or values.

Common Family Vision™
In the context of family businesses, creating a Common Family Vision™ is a way of making a promise or resolution to contribute to the common good of the family. The Common Family Vision™ is created out of those values a family wants to see perpetuated in their business. These high-level principles are discussed and developed

into a brief paragraph that truly reflects what the family believes about themselves and their values. Some families think of them as mission statements. I've found this Common Family Vision™ to be key for happier, healthier families.

Entrepreneur's Checklist™

_____ 1. Economic security—share with your spouse

_____ 2. Create an ownership plan to transfer ownership and control of the business

_____ 3. Create an estate plan that is communicated to your family

_____ 4. Create and train the new leadership team

_____ 5. Develop a Life Career Plan™ with your spouse

_____ 6. Create an active board of advisors

_____ 7. Codify your family's heritage and stories

_____ 8. Provide leadership to celebrate family rituals

_____ 9. Support family meetings

_____ 10. Create a Common Family Vision™

_____ 11. Create a leadership plan for the adult children working in the company

_____ 12. Identify and celebrate your family values

_____ 13. Create a family philanthropy and services plan for your family

_____ 14. Create a Family Participation Plan™

_____ 15. Assist in creating career plans for adult children who are not in the family business

_____ 16. Create an ethical will

Shareholder's Code of Conduct Checklist™

_____ 1. With regard to the family business, make a commitment to understand the business of the business with a philosophy of "noses in, fingers out."

_____ 2. Continue to work on your life purpose and manifest it to the best of your ability in your chosen career.

_____ 3. Make a commitment to understand the company financials and develop financial literacy.

_____ 4. Work with your family council to establish appropriate expectations for the performance of the company.

_____ 5. Be part of a team to create and maintain a governance process for the business.

_____ 6. Consistent with the culture of your family, openly and genuinely share your appreciation and love for one another.

_____ 7. Make a commitment to confidentiality in regard to everything related to the business, financials, and anything discussed in family meetings or in your own family.

_____ 8. Be able to manage your relation to money so as to create financial wellbeing in your life.

_____ 9. Whenever possible, always participate in family rituals, family events, and family meetings designed to celebrate the family.

_____ 10. Have a reciprocal commitment to one another's success.

_____ 11. Be able to speak your truth without judgment, criticism, or blame.

12. Make a commitment to have the direct discussion of issues and a win-win philosophy of managing differences.

13. When hurts or transgressions occur, be willing to forgive one another and create a new beginning.

14. When circumstances require it, be prepared to make a contribution to the common good out of your love, your generosity, your sense of abundance, and the trust that if I make a contribution now, others will do so when their turn comes.

15. Given the blessings of your life, develop a commitment to service and philanthropy that reflects the gratitude you have for your blessings.

Shareholders, Directors, and Officers

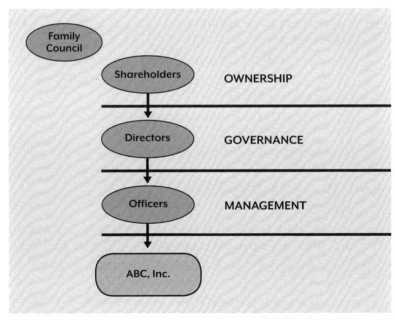

Adapted from the model developed by Glen Ayres

Four Different Roles

Shareholders/Family Council
- Need for a forum to discuss family concerns
  - Includes all family, not just those owning stock
  - Address family issues
    - > Training
    - > Employment policies
    - > Family stock ownership policies
  - Keep informed about the company and the business
  - Keep board of directors informed on family goals
    - > Family vision
    - > Annual priorities
- Normally followed by a short shareholder meeting for those who actually own stock
  - Elect directors
  - Discuss and vote on any corporate action requiring shareholder approval

Shareholders <u>Own</u> the Corporation
- Shareholders Do . . .
  - Vote to elect a competent board of directors
  - Let the board of directors know what their goals are
- Shareholders Do Not . . .
  - Set basic policies for the business
  - Hire, compensate, or evaluate officers
  - Manage the business

Directors Govern the Corporation
- Directors Do . . .
  - Set basic policies through the strategic planning process
  - Hire, evaluate, and compensate senior management
  - Monitor whether basic policies are being followed
- Directors Do Not . . .
  - Manage the business
  - Elect themselves

Officers Manage the Corporation

- Officers Do . . .
  - Run the day-to-day operations
  - Develop strategic plans and budgets for submission to the board
  - Implement strategic plans and budgets approved by the board
  - Report to the board

- Officers Do Not . . .
  - Set basic policies for the business
  - Hire, compensate, or evaluate themselves
  - Elect the directors

Areas of Work in Family-Owned Businesses

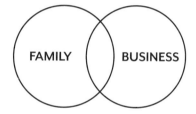

FAMILY ISSUES
- Communication & Management Differences
- Closeness & Intimacy
- Relationship
- In-laws
- Expectations
- Significance

FAMILY MEETING
- Common Vision
- Individual Vision
- Commitment to each other's success
- Reconciliation

OWNERSHIP PLAN
- Ownership Plan
- Estate Plan
- Board & Governance Plan

MANAGEMENT & LEADERSHIP
- Career Plan
- Leadership Plan & Coaching
- Decision Making System
- Compensation Plan
- Transition from Entrepreneurial Company

BUSINESS PLAN
- Strategic Business Plan
- Create Net Worth

Challenges

Ownership

- The Last Challenge of Entrepreneurship™
- One owner to multiple owners
- Liquidity plan for owner
- Leadership
- Wealth and money concern

Suggested Actions

- Board – Governance
- Estate plan
- Cost of business and education/ architect of the new governance system
- Wealth Preparation Planning

Management & Leadership

- Leadership
- Compensation issues
- Letting go
- Who does what?

Suggested Actions

- Planning & Training
- Creating an objective system
- Life/Career Planning™
- Structure Organization

Business Plan

- Continue business success
- Buy-out of senior generation
- Measuring stick to evaluate company performance
- Leadership of business by next generation
- Net worth

Suggested Actions

- Strategic plan
- Strategic plan
- Strategic plan

- Strategic plan as measuring stick

- Strategic plan

Family

- Maintain family relationship without undue influence of the business
    Parent/child
    Unity
    Rituals
- Management of differences
    Expectations
    Role of in-laws

Suggested Actions

- Family meetings
- Common Family Vision™

- Family meetings
- Family meetings
- Family meetings

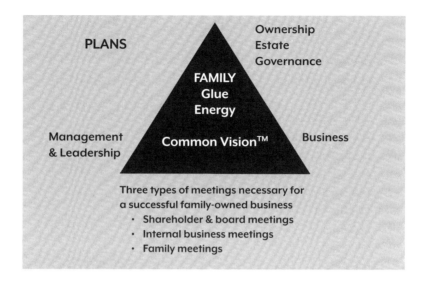

Three types of meetings necessary for
a successful family-owned business
- Shareholder & board meetings
- Internal business meetings
- Family meetings

FAMILY MEETINGS

- **Family Values – the building blocks**
- **Common Family Vision™ – the family united by the common dream**
    - Individual visions – give a sense of purpose
    - Family Rituals – the glue that holds the family together

- **Focus of family meetings**
    - Issues of change
    - Issues of loss
    - Issues of expectations
    - Dreams/Family rituals
    - Family relationships
    - Family issues and transitions
    - Business issues and transitions
    - Overlap
    - Strengthen family relationships
    - Build the emotional equity of the family

- **Family Skills – behaviors necessary for success**
    - Talking – sharing
    - Listening – understanding
    - Management of differences – problem solving
    - Forgiveness – reconciliation

COMMON FAMILY BUSINESS CONCERNS

- Family harmony
- Family relationships
- Family rituals
- Communication
- Management of differences
- Expression of emotions
- Appreciation, recognition, and celebration
- Overlap between family and business
- Influence of work
- Competence
- Competition
- Money
- Compensation
- Equality
- Control
- Ownership
- Letting go
- Career plan
- Change
- Inclusion
- Generational

Twenty-three Ways to Deal with the Tough Stuff in Family Business™

1. Have well-established guidelines for entry into the family business.

2. Establish clear expectations and guidelines for performance.

3. Develop career-training programs to assist family members in achieving their goals.

4. Consider appointing a mentor to assist the younger generation with career plans.

5. Use an industrial psychologist to establish career plans for the younger generation.

6. Establish a Life Career Plan™.

7. Have direct discussions about issues, and avoid Hubler's Speck of Dust Theory™.

8. Balance the expression of your feelings and wants with thought about the issue.

9. Use Sherod Miller's **B.O.S.S.** concept as an organizing principle in all discussions.

10. Use the "O" part of the **B.O.S.S.** to openly promote the success of what the other wants.

11. Create a decision-making system that honors the **B.O.S.S.**

12. Be a vision-driven family-owned business as opposed to problem-focused.

13. Use the Common Family Vision™ to unite the family in regard to the business.

14. Have semi-annual family meetings to assist in the balance of family and business.

15. In order to maintain balance between family and business, establish plans in the following areas:

- Ownership and estate
- Management and leadership
- Business
- Family

16. Create an active board with outside advisors.

17. Use the board or outside advisors to establish a compensation plan.

18. When it comes to change, acknowledge your part of the issue, and don't try to change others.

19. When hurt and misunderstandings occur, use forgiveness and reconciliation to bring you back to balance.

20. Openly and regularly acknowledge the positive qualities of the other.

21. Openly celebrate your rituals and successes.

22. Create space and time for relationships outside the business, and make an investment in your emotional bank account. The accumulated investment can be drawn upon later to deal with the tough stuff.

23. Use H.E.A.R.T.[i] to assist your dialogues:
   - **H**ear and understand me (listen)
   - **E**ven if you disagree, please don't make me wrong
   - **A**cknowledge the greatness within me
   - **R**emember to look for my loving intentions
   - **T**ell me the truth with compassion

The Life Career Planning Program™

"Life can only be understood backwards,
but it must be lived forwards."
Soren Kierkegaard

Backing into the future is always precarious. The "golden years" have the potential to be the best of our lives, yet most people fail to plan for their later years. The ambiguity of not having a plan creates unnecessary and unproductive anxiety. Even though our life expectancy has increased significantly, few people know how to use the later years in a meaningful way. The goal of the Life Career Planning Program™ is to help individuals integrate their life experiences in order to transform knowledge into wisdom and live their lives to the fullest.

The Life Career Planning Program™ is designed to assist couples in creating their lives and their futures as they want them. We focus the action planning on seven key areas of discovery:

- Work
- Money/wealth
- Relationships
- Community service
- Leisure time
- Health
- Spirituality

Program Overview

Phase One: Harvesting
The goal of this phase is to help clients to:

1. Celebrate the blessings in their life
2. Honor and let go of the regrets and hurts of the past

We assist clients to integrate the polarity of life and death and come to terms with the present realities in their family and/or business. Through harvesting the past, clients will be able to stand in the present and make choices about what they want for their family in the future. We take clients through a process of forgiveness and healing that includes both assessment and action planning.

Phase One consists of three half-day meetings with the couple: two for reviewing the past and one for discussion and action planning for the future. Multiple activities will be used in this phase including interview, visualization, facilitated discussions, journal writing, and development activities designed to enhance their goals.

Phase Two: Turning the Soil

During Phase Two we facilitate discussion about the client's purpose and meaning in life, the role spirituality plays in their work and life, and how to achieve happiness through aligning one's gifts in all the above areas of life.

Phase Two consists of two hour-long confidential coaching sessions with each spouse focused on the development and manifestation of their personal gifts.

Phase Three: Planting New Seeds

During Phase Three we assist clients in the creation of their plan for the future based on the values and goals they have articulated and the development they have begun in Phases One and Two. Strategies will be outlined for how to take action in each of the seven areas of life and ensure future harvests.

Phase Three consists of two half-day meetings with the couple, plus a six-month review.

Benefits

Participants in the program will receive the following benefits:

- A clear plan for meaningful work and leisure time
- A sense of fulfillment and purpose
- A united perspective on values
- Converting their dreams into reality
- Peace of mind
- The skills to communicate goals to others

Questions

When thinking about your plans for the future, ask yourself the following questions:

1. What are your seven most important beliefs?

2. What are the ten major stepping-stones of your life?

3. How have these events shaped your life and influenced you in regard to your life plan?

4. What are the major strengths you have developed as a result of your life experiences?

5. What are your spiritual gifts?

6. What is your purpose in life?

    - What are your talents?
    - What are you really passionate about?
    - What is the most natural environment for your life?
    - Identify the most important elements of the three previous questions and combine them into a sentence that goes as follows: "My purpose in life is _____."

7. What is my dream in relation to:

    - Work
    - Family
    - Leisure
    - Service
    - Philanthropy
    - Health
    - Purpose
    - Personal mastery

After answering these questions, use your answers to develop an action plan for this next phase of your life.

From the Gregg Levoy Seminar:
Callings—The Power of Passion at Work

Tom's Note: I attended an excellent workshop by Gregg Levoy, speaker and author of *Vital Signs: Discovering and Sustaining Your Passion for Life* and *Callings: Finding and Following an Authentic Life.* The following list of questions comes from *Callings: Finding and Following an Authentic Life*[ii]. The second question is my favorite.

1. At the end of your life, if you are walking with an angel on your way to heaven and the angel said to you, "What did you like best about it?" How would you answer?

2. What is the one question you were born to answer?

3. What subject(s) can you speak about with real authority?

4. What wishes would you ask for if you had three wishes? You cannot ask for any more wishes.

5. Granted the opportunity to have three mentors, who would they be and why?

6. If you had an hour's worth of primetime TV what would you talk about?

7. If you knew that you could not fail, what would you undertake now?

8. What is the most important thing missing from your life right now?

9. If it takes a little chaos to strengthen and shake a person up or to create change, what small bit of chaos would you introduce right now to strengthen and help your life evolve?

10. What have you rejected in your life that continues to claim you?

11. What pattern in your life are you absolutely sick of?

12. The unlived life of our parents is a very powerful concept and to some extent influences our choices. To the degree that you are aware of, what are the unlived aspects of each of your parents and what effect have they had on you?

13. What has been your most memorable break with tradition?

14. Name someone who is living a life that inspires you.

15. Name someone you know who is furthest from following his or her own sense of calling or authenticity.

16. What is the single greatest regret of your life?

17. What is the most important affirmation put up in your home or your office?

18. What is the most consistent internal message in the last year related to your work?

Circle any reoccurring words or themes that stand out to you as you review your responses to the 18 questions.

19. Choose something to focus on for today that you would like to develop.

Resistance
1. Name the demons of your life that stop you from accomplishing what you'd like to do.

2. Albert Ellis talks about the impact of other people, the scandalization of others, and the difficulty we all have in being true to ourselves. The question is, what are other people going to say about you following the call of your life that is negative?

3. There's always a shadow in every call, and Thomas Moore talks about it in some of his works. What is it you will have to give up to accomplish your calling?

4. Based on the experiences working with people over the years, many people who are unable to achieve their goals act based on the assumption that there's something unacceptable about them that holds them back. The notion here is that there is a core wound. Do you have a core wound or something that

happened to you as a child that wasn't your fault? Retell the story of your life with the wound as the middle of your life, not the end.

Affirmative

1. What are the voices of yes or the arguments in favor of your calling?

2. Write a list of resources that can help support you, push you toward action, and be a source of inspiration to you.

3. What are the payoffs of accomplishing your calling?

4. What are the acknowledgments that would help inspire you to claim your calling and accomplish it?

5. The single most important characteristic of a successful company or person is being able to hold two paradoxical things at the same time. Take a moment to identify the calling of your life and have a written dialogue between the voice of yes and the voice of no. Name those voices and use them to further identify the issue in your life related to your calling. The idea is to spontaneously write for a half hour anything that comes to your mind relative to this dialogue.

Tom Hubler's Recommended Readings

* *Let Your Life Speak* by Parker Palmer

* *The Power of Purpose* by Richard Leider

Whistle While You Work by Richard Leider

Repacking Your Bags by Richard Leider and David A. Shapiro

Claiming Your Place at the Fire: Living the Second Half of Your Life on Purpose by Richard Leider and David Shapiro

Finding Flow by Mihaly Csikszentmihalyi

The Soul's Code by James Hillman

Sacred Contracts: Awakening Your Divine Potential by Caroline Myss

Callings: Finding and Following an Authentic Life by Gregg LeVoy

* *The Congruent Life* by C. Michael Thompson

Hearing with the Heart: A Gentle Guide for Discerning God's Will for Your Life by Debra K. Farrington

Life Launch by Frederic Hudson

The Purpose Driven Life by Rick Warren

Paths Are Made By Walking: Practical Steps for Attaining Serenity by Therese Jacobs-Stewart

* *Hidden Wholeness* by Parker Palmer

Now, Discover Your Strengths by Marcus Buckingham and Donald O. Clifton

* *The Second Half of Life: Opening the Eight Gates of Wisdom* by Angeles Arrien

(* denotes Tom's favorites)

References

Foreword

[i] Oxford Dictionaries, s.v. "soul," https://en.oxforddictionaries.com/definition/soul.

[ii] Astrachan, J. H., and M. C. Shanker. "Family Businesses' Contribution to the U.S. Economy: A Closer Look," *Family Business Review*, no. 16 (2003): 211-219. https://digitalcommons.kennesaw.edu/facpubs/2373/.

[iii] Miller, S. *Collaborative Team Skills.* Interpersonal Communication Programs Inc., 2005 (first published 1994).

Chapter 1

[i] Chethik, N. *Fatherloss: How Sons of All Ages Come to Terms with the Deaths of Their Dads.* New York: Hachette Books, 2001.

[ii] Astrachan, J. H., and M. C. Shanker. "Family Businesses' Contribution to the U.S. Economy: A Closer Look," *Family Business Review*, no. 16 (2003): 211-219. https://digitalcommons.kennesaw.edu/facpubs/2373/.

[iii] Astrachan, J. H., and M. C. Shanker. "Family Businesses' Contribution to the U.S. Economy: A Closer Look," *Family Business Review*, no. 16 (2003): 211-219. https://digitalcommons.kennesaw.edu/facpubs/2373/.

[iv] Schwass, J., et al. *Wise Wealth: Creating It, Managing It, Preserving It.* Palgrave Macmillan Ltd., 2010.

[v] Miller, S. *Collaborative Team Skills.* Interpersonal Communication Programs Inc., 2005 (first published 1994).

Chapter 2

[i] Sherrill, M. "The Buddha of Detroit." *The New York Times*, November 26, 2000. http://partners.nytimes.com/library/magazine/home/20001126mag-ford.html.

[ii] Whyte, D. *The Heart Aroused.* Bantam Doubleday Dell Publishing Group, 1994.

iii Miller, S. *Collaborative Team Skills*. Interpersonal Communication Programs Inc., 2005 (first published 1994).

iv Csikszentmihalyi, M. *Finding Flow: The Psychology of Engagement With Everyday Life*, 110-113. Basic Books, 1997.

v Straub, G. *Rhythm of Compassion: Caring for Self Connecting With Society*. Empowerment Institute, 2008.

vi Peck, M. S. *A Road Less Travelled: A New Psychology of Love, Traditional Values, and Spiritual Growth*. Arrow New-Age, 1990 (first published 1978).

vii Arrien, A. *The Four-fold Way: Walking the Paths of the Warrior, Teacher, Healer and Visionary*. HarperCollins, 2013.

viii Autry, J. A. *Choosing Gratitude: Learning to Love the Life You Have*. Macon, GA: Smyth & Helwys Pub, 2012.

ix Arrien, A. *Living in Gratitude: A Journey That Will Change Your Life*. Boulder, CO: Sounds True, 2011.

x Emmons, R. A. *Thanks!: How the New Science of Gratitude Can Make You Happier*. Boston: Houghton Mifflin Co., 2007.

Chapter 3

i Shatkin, L. *150 Best Low-Stress Jobs*. Indianapolis, IN: JIST Works, 2008.

ii Sood, A. *SMART* (Stress Management and Resiliency Training). http://stressfree.org/programs/smart/.

iii Kabat-Zinn, M., and J. Kabat-Zinn. *Everyday Blessings: The Inner Work of Mindful Parenting*. New York: Hyperion, 1997.

iv Miller, S. *Collaborative Team Skills*. Interpersonal Communication Programs Inc., 2005 (first published 1994).

Chapter 4

i Miller, D. P. *A Little Book of Forgiveness*. Viking Press, 1994.

ii Nash, L. L., and S. McLennan. *Church on Sunday, Work on Monday: The Challenge of Fusing Christian Values with Business Life, a Guide to*

Reflection. San Francisco, CA: Jossey-Bass, 2001.

[iii] Miller, S. *Collaborative Team Skills*. Interpersonal Communication Programs Inc., 2005 (first published 1994).

[iv] Luskin, F. *Forgive for Good*. HarperCollins, 2003.

[v] Ryback, T. W. *The Last Survivor: Legacies of Dachau*. New York: Vintage, 2000.

[vi] Schachter-Shalomi, Z., and R. S. Miller. *From Age-ing to Sage-ing: A Profound New Vision of Growing Older*. New York: Warner Books.

[vii] McClendon, R., and L. Kadis. *Reconciling Relationships and Preserving the Family Business: Tools for Success.* New York: Haworth Press, 2004.

[viii] Miller, D. P. *A Little Book of Forgiveness*. Viking Press, 1994.

[ix] Kornfield, J. *The Art of Forgiveness, Lovingkindness, and Peace.* New York: Bantam Books, 2002.

[x] Nash, L., and H. Stevenson. "Success That Lasts," *Harvard Business Review*, February 2004. https://hbr.org/2004/02/success-that-lasts.

[xi] Csikszentmihalyi, M. *Finding Flow: The Psychology of Engagement with Everyday Life*. Basic Books, 1997.

[xii] Miller, S., and P. Miller. *Collaborative Team Skills*. Interpersonal Communication, 1994.

[xiii] Poza, E. J. *Family Business*. 3rd ed. South-Western College Pub, 2009.

Chapter 5

[i] Miller, S., and P. Miller. *Collaborative Team Skills*. Interpersonal Communication, 1994.

[ii] Myers, P., and K. D. Myers. *Myers-Briggs Type Indicator*. Palo Alto, CA: Consulting Psychologists Press, 1977.

[iii] Straub, G., and D. Gershon. "Empowerment Workshop." Empowerment Institute. http://www.empowermentinstitute.net/index.php/

personal/empowerment-workshop.

iv Coontz, S. *The Way We Never Were: American Families and the Nostalgia Trap*. New York: Basic Books, 1993.

v Kabat-Zinn, J. *Full Catastrophe Living*. New York: Delacorte Press, 1990.

vi Miller, D. P. *A Little Book of Forgiveness*. Viking Press, 1994.

vii Jaworski, J. *Synchronicity: The Inner Path of Leadership*. San Francisco, CA: Berrewt-Koehler Publisher, 1996.

viii Poza, E. J. *Family Business*. 3rd ed. South-Western College Pub, 2009.

ix Astrachan, J. H., and M. C. Shanker. "Family Businesses' Contribution to the U.S. Economy: A Closer Look," *Family Business Review*, no. 16 (2003): 211-219. https://digitalcommons.kennesaw.edu/fac-pubs/2373/.

x Collins, J. *Good to Great: Why Some Companies Make the Leap . . . And Others Don't*. HarperBusiness, 2011.

xi Csikszentmihalyi, M. *Finding Flow: The Psychology of Engagement with Everyday Life*. Basic Books, 1997.

xii Palmer, P. J. *Let Your Life Speak: Listening for the Voice of Vocation*. San Francisco, CA: Jossey-Bass, 2009.

xiii Dungan, N. *Prodigal Sons and Material Girls: How Not to Become Your Child's ATM*. Wiley, 2003.

xiv Thompson, C. M. *The Congruent Life: Following the Inward Path to Fulfilling Work and Inspired Leadership*. San Francisco, CA: Jossey-Bass, 2000.

Chapter 6

i Nash, L., and H. H. Stevenson. "Success That Lasts," *Harvard Business Review*, February 2004. https://hbr.org/2004/02/success-that-lasts.

ⁱⁱ Allianz American Legacies. "Discoveries of the American Legacies White Paper," *Discoveries of the American Legacies White Paper,* 2005. https://www.allianzlife.com/-/media/files/allianz/documents/ent_120_n.pdf.

Chapter 7

ⁱ Conger, J. A., & Associates. *Spirit at Work.* Chap. 2, "Leading from Within: Out of the Shadow, into the Light," by Parker Palmer. San Francisco, CA: Jossey-Bass, 1994.

ⁱⁱ Whyte, D. "Beowulf – Power and Vulnerability in the Workplace." In *The Heart Aroused.* New York: Doubleday Publishers, 1996.

ⁱⁱⁱ Senge, P. *The Fifth Discipline: The Art and Practice of the Learning Organization.* New York: Doubleday Publishers, 1990.

ⁱᵛ Myers, P., and K. D. Myers. *Myers-Briggs Type Indicator.* Palo Alto, CA: Consulting Psychologists Press, 1977.

Afterword

ⁱ Miller, S. *Collaborative Team Skills,* Interpersonal Communication Programs Inc., 2005 (first published 1994).

Appendix

ⁱ Bracey, H. J., J. Rosenblum, A. Sanford, and R. Trueblood. *Managing from the Heart.* New York: Dell, 1993.

ⁱⁱ Levoy, G. *Callings: Finding and Following an Authentic Life.* Harmony, 1998.